DEAR ALEC

Drawing by Clive Francis
Key on page 121

DEAR ALEC
GUINNESS AT 75

EDITED BY
RONALD HARWOOD

LIMELIGHT EDITIONS 1989
NEW YORK

THIS IS A LIMELIGHT EDITION
PUBLISHED BY PROSCENIUM PUBLISHERS, INC.

Copyright in the compilation © 1989 by
Ronald Harwood and Hodder and Stoughton.
Copyright in the Introduction © 1989 by
Ronald Harwood. Copyright in the articles
© 1989 by the contributors. Copyright in the
frontispiece © 1989 by Clive Francis.

First Edition

Library of Congress Cataloging-in-Publication Data

Dear Alec: Guinness at 75/edited by Ronald Harwood. – 1st ed
   Limelight ed.
      p.   cm.
   Includes index.
   ISBN 0-87910-127-X
      1. Guinness, Alec, 1914–   2. Actors – Great Britain –
   I. Harwood, Ronald, 1934–
   PN2598.G8D4   1989
   792'.028'092—dc20
   [B]   89-3397'
                                                         CIP

Photoset by Rowland Phototypesetting Ltd,
Bury St Edmunds, Suffolk.

Printed in Great Britain by St Edmundsbury Press Ltd,
Bury St Edmunds, Suffolk.

CONTENTS

ILLUSTRATIONS

Between pages 120 and 121

The Cardinal in *The Prisoner*, 1954.[3]
Hamlet, 1951.[8]
Jock Sinclair in *Tunes of Glory*, 1960.[3]
Lawrence in *Ross*, 1960.[3]
Ben Kenobi in *Star Wars*, 1977.[3]
From the portrait in oils by Michael Noakes, 1971.[4]
William Dorrit in *Little Dorrit*, 1986.[5]
The Pope in *Brother Sun, Sister Moon*, 1973.[3]
George Smiley, 1979 and 1981.[3]
Andrey Brotvinnik in *A Walk in the Woods*, 1988.[9]

1. Alec Guinness
2. Mander and Mitchenson Theatre Collection
3. The Kobal Collection
4. Michael Noakes
5. Sands Films (Dorrit) Ltd
6. The Rank Organisation plc
7. John Vickers Archive
8. Houston Rogers
9. Donald Cooper

INTRODUCTION

Ronald Harwood was born in South Africa in 1934, and came to England in 1951. He is author of several novels and a biography of Sir Donald Wolfit. His plays include *A Family*, *The Ordeal of Gilbert Pinfold*, *The Dresser* (for which he subsequently wrote the screenplay), *Tramway Road*, *Interpreters* and *J. J. Farr*. He also edited *The Ages of Gielgud*.

INTRODUCTION
RONALD HARWOOD

The most persistent myth surrounding Alec Guinness is that his quality as an actor depends on his anonymity as a person. How, the argument runs, can an actor who so completely changes personality with each part he plays have any personality of his own?

In all that has been written about him, in books, articles and critical studies, the recurring theme may be summed up by the journalists whose pieces all seem to be headlined: 'Is this the *real* Alec Guinness?' The variations are endless: 'The quiet one they call him' . . . 'The man with so many faces on the screen that in private life no one recognises him' . . . The preoccupation is shared by his public and, to some extent, his fellow-professionals. So varied are his performances, so thorough his impersonations that the man himself remains invisible. It is possible, or so it seems to me, to detect in other actors, even when playing heavily disguised characters, something of their private personas or, if that is too great a claim, a recognisable presence, mannerisms at least, tricks of voice and diction. But Guinness does not fit that mould, hence the oft-asked question, 'What's he really like?'

This book, then, is a modest attempt to answer that question, to try and catch a glimpse, no more, of the private person whose seventy-fifth birthday his friends and colleagues take such pleasure in celebrating.

One has to begin with Guinness, the actor, because it is the actor who lays so many false trails. I know this from personal experience.

'You must see Alec Guinness in his new film,' someone once said. 'He is absolutely amazing. No, I'm not going to tell you any more because it'll spoil the surprise.' On a hot summer's day in November 1949, as a fifteenth birthday treat to myself, I went off to the local bioscope, the Adelphi in Sea Point, Cape Town, to see Valerie Hobson, Dennis Price, Joan Greenwood and Alec Guinness in *Kind Hearts and Coronets*, a Michael Balcon production for Ealing Films, directed by Robert Hamer, the story of a young man who kills off all the eight heirs who stand between him and his inheritance. A hilarious study, the poster announced, in the gentle art of MURDER. I watched the film. I was disappointed. I couldn't understand what all the fuss was about. The young man seemed to me good but not particularly brilliant. But then, I came out thinking that Alec Guinness was Dennis Price. It was only a week later I learned that Guinness had played all eight heirs. He had fooled me. I saw the film again. I was awed but mildly resentful.

I could say it was my first impression of him but the truth is I had countless first impressions of him. Each time I saw him, in films, later in the theatre, I had the uncanny feeling I had never before watched him act. His personality, if indeed he had one, was somehow obliterated by the part he played. I saw him as Fagin in *Oliver Twist*, but how could that actor, with his grotesque nose and dank beard, with his lilting, 'Awliver, my dear,' be the same one who played the entire d'Ascoyne family in *Kind Hearts and Coronets*? I saw him next in *Last Holiday*, a film based on an original screenplay by J. B. Priestley. Now, this was more like it: no beard, no moustache, no false nose, no accent, a rather meek sort of chap, this surely must be the real Alec Guinness. That view may have been confirmed by the character he played in *The Lavender Hill Mob*, Henry Holland, archetype of the little man who turns out to be rather bigger than anyone expected. But then with each succeeding film or play the assessment of Guinness the actor had, and still has, to be revised which makes the private man all the more elusive. If one were to attempt to piece together a personality from the parts played you end up with a face difficult to describe, a kindly man, no, not exactly kindly, a touch severe, no, meek, perhaps, well, no, not exactly meek, inoffensive rather, benign with a glint of steel. That must be the real Alec Guinness: a severe, benign, steely cypher. No, that can't be true, or can it? Is his personality really obliterated by the parts he plays? In the doubt lies a clue.

Guinness, the over-rated Kenneth Tynan[1] once asserted, belongs to no tradition. In this, as in so many things, he was entirely wrong. Guinness's theatrical ancestry is ancient and pure and provides yet further clues to the artist and the man. In the golden age of Athens, around 500 BC, the theatre was central to the life and well-being of the city. The buildings themselves were made of wood; the religious connection to Dionysus, the god of the theatre, was strong and sincere; actors, all male, performed in masks which were never removed, not even to acknowledge the audience's approval at the end of the performance. It was only later, when Athens was in decline, that the vast auditoria we know today were built, clad in marble and lavishly decorated to proclaim the city's decadence; lip-service was paid to the religious impulse; actors continued to wear masks but at the end of the performance removed them so that the public could see (and later recognise) the men who wore them. In his so-called private life the actor became a public figure, strutted the streets, was pointed at, admired, sought after, his name known to the populace; thus, the first star system was born.

Now, Guinness by temperament, inclination and gift pays allegiance to the tradition of the anonymous Athenian actor who never removed the mask, but, uncomfortably for him, he lives and works in an age to which this idea is alien and suspect. Our new London playhouses are vast, elaborate edifices whose foyers are often larger than the auditoria; to talk of a religious dimension in the contemporary theatre is ludicrous; the actor is an honoured, celebrated member of society. The assertion of ego is so much a part of our daily lives that, especially in actors, concepts of modesty, humility, sense of service are viewed either with contempt or disbelief. In Guinness his artistic preference is at odds with the demands of the world into which he was born and that has created an internal conflict which is at the very root of his talent and personality. Both are governed by a demon who alternates between servant and master, unassuming and self-assertive, spiritual and earth-bound, meek and incredibly powerful.

As with most leading actors, Guinness's talent and personality are formidable and indivisible. In private his presence is as compelling as it is on stage or screen, but he seems able to enhance or diminish the effect of his presence at will. If he wishes to make his

---

[1] Dramatic critic (1927–80); author of *Alec Guinness* (Rockliff, London, 1953).

presence felt it is, believe me, felt; if he wishes to be recognised he is recognised. It is also true that he is neither handsome nor plain, an unremarkable-looking man which makes instant recognition difficult. His face has been described as 'pleasantly bland' – but then, so, too, from all accounts, was David Garrick's, the first great star of the English theatre. The trick is, however, not to confuse the parts Guinness plays and his physical appearance with his persona.

That ability to command his personality may be more easily appreciated in a book Guinness published in 1985 which was described as an autobiography. Yet, he, the autobiographer is strangely absent. At first glance the book is really about the people who have mattered to him, who exerted an influence on his life and career. The reader has to work hard to gain an impression of the writer. With application, however, it is possible to detect certain attributes: he has acute powers of observation, a keen intelligence and a vivid memory for people. But, unlike most autobiographies, the author keeps his distance, as if writing about someone who doesn't really matter and who can be of no possible interest to anyone. It is little wonder, therefore, that the book is called Blessings in Disguise[1] and that, in his introduction, he replaces the personal pronoun with the word 'ego'. 'Enter EGO from the wings,' it begins, 'pursued by fiends. Exit EGO.' All this stems, I believe, from his love of concealment which is intriguing, mischievous and irksome. In private, he has a way of wrong-footing one, of being contrary, of always seeming to withhold part of himself. It is his right, of course. He is a great actor and great actors have to learn to use their personalities, the raw material of their art, sparingly.

There is another factor to be taken into account when considering the elusiveness of Alec Guinness, the private person. In many of the contributions to this book, attention is drawn to the actor's modesty. When Ion Trewin, the publisher, and I approached Guinness to discuss this book with him, he was genuinely reluctant to have anything to do with it[2]. He did not want his friends bothered, he said at first, but later in the conversation let slip, 'I can understand a book of this kind about Olivier or Gielgud but not me.' We then had to explain that he was generally regarded

---

[1] Published by Hamish Hamilton, London, 1985.
[2] See the epilogue.

throughout the world as a leading English actor, much loved by his audiences, his colleagues and his friends who would like nothing more than to celebrate publicly his seventy-fifth birthday. This revelation caused him to wince. His embarrassment was real and acute. Reluctantly, he gave his permission for us to proceed provided we did not bother him again. This trait, exemplified repeatedly and in a variety of ways in the pieces that follow, may seem to some an affectation. To the outsider, it may be incomprehensible that anyone, especially an actor, so famous and acclaimed, should for a moment doubt his own importance or, professionally, so lack in confidence. But it is that very self-doubt, that lack of confidence, that reticence which makes him endearing and the nonpareil of actors.

It is tempting – at least, it is to me – to play amateur psychiatrist, to try to find in his background the forces that moulded this man who is superbly gifted, kindly, severe, painfully honest, lavishly hospitable, courageous, concealed, persistent and maddeningly modest. He himself is similarly tempted:

> Many actors, when they have made a name for themselves, are endlessly recounting in the public prints how they don't know who they are, why they are, or, indeed, where they are . . . I . . . was born to confusion and totally immersed in it for several years, owning three different names until the age of fourteen and living in about thirty different hotels, lodgings and flats, each of which was hailed as 'home' until such time as my mother and I flitted, leaving behind, like a paper-chase, a wake of unpaid bills.

He was born in Marylebone, London on April 2nd, 1914, and he was illegitimate or, as he preferred to describe it to American television viewers, a love child. His mother's name was Miss Agnes Cuffe and his father, whom he met only four or five times and was taught to call uncle, was a Scot named Andrew, a bank director, aged sixty-four when Alec was born. He apparently made barely adequate financial contributions so that Agnes could bring up her son in a variety of lodgings in genteel poverty. First, Alec was called de Cuffe, then Striven in deference to a stepfather whom he hated, and lastly, aged fourteen, Guinness.

According to one of his biographers, John Russell Taylor[1], Alec

[1] *Alec Guinness – A Celebration* (Pavilion, London, 1984).

seemed as a child 'a quiet, well-behaved, rather solitary observer.'
Aged six, he was sent off to boarding school, Normandale at
Bexhill-on-Sea, and a talent for mimicry and story-telling was soon
revealed. This may have made him special to the other boys but he
thought of himself as merely 'odd' and 'unprepossessing'. Yet, he
auditioned for the school dramatic society, convinced the head-
master that he had no talent whatsoever and was, as a result, rejected.

His second school, Roxborough, was a private establishment
near Eastbourne and here he made his first appearance on any
stage, playing a messenger in *Macbeth*. He also displayed a gift for
writing so that when he left school he joined an advertising agency,
Arks Publicity, for whom he wrote copy (Rose's Lime Juice,
Mullard's Radio Valves and Wilkinson's Razor Blades) and was
paid £1 a week. He lived alone in Westbourne Grove and spent all
his spare cash on going to the theatre. In time, the conviction grew
that he wanted to become an actor – 'I just wanted to be someone
else, to be in make-up, in disguise.'

John Gielgud was his hero and, according to John Russell Taylor,
young Alec, with the extraordinary impudence of youth, simply
telephoned the great actor and asked for advice. Gielgud, who has
a wonderful way of taking things in his stride, advised voice lessons
from Martita Hunt, and Alec Guinness was on his way. He tried
RADA next but needed a scholarship which was not forthcoming
and his path led eventually to a private drama school run by a
distinguished London actress, Fay Compton. He made his first
professional appearance as a junior counsel in *Libel!* by Edward
Wooll at the Playhouse Theatre on his twentieth birthday, April
2nd, 1934. By the end of that year he was playing Osric to John
Gielgud's Hamlet at the New (now the Albery) Theatre and his
career was launched.

Guinness had the rare good fortune – like John Gielgud – of
never having to play in provincial repertory or in second-rate
tours, of never having to go through the conventional tread-
mill. From the start, he performed in work of high quality
alongside leading members of the English theatre: Gielgud,
Michel Saint-Denis[1], Theodore Komisarjevsky[2], Tyrone

---

[1] Director and teacher (1897–1971) who exerted an important influence on the
English stage.
[2] Russian-born director (1882–1954) who worked in England and Western
Europe from 1919.

Guthrie[1], Laurence Olivier, Robert Newton, Edith Evans, Peggy Ashcroft. By the time war was declared in 1939, he was a leading actor, at least at the Old Vic, and beginning to make his mark. He married Merula Salaman in 1938, and three years later, their only child, Matthew was born.

After serving in the Royal Navy[2], he unpacked his make-up case and carried on more or less where he left off. But it was the cinema that was to transform his career once and for all. His first screen appearance was as Herbert Pocket in *Great Expectations* directed by David Lean; since then he has appeared in films which range from *The Ladykillers* to *The Bridge on the River Kwai*, from *The Man in the White Suit* to *Star Wars*. The cinema proclaimed his phenomenal range as an actor and brought him world fame.

But Guinness never deserted the theatre for long. He may spend a few years making films but inevitably he seems to feel the need to return to the stage. In both media, his technique is anti-rhetorical. I suspect he abhors the idea of 'great acting' with all it implies. In every sense he is a modern actor who strives for realism. Sometimes, he can stray too much in this direction and seem impersonal, oblique, unfocused. But when the character he plays matches his style – and this can be in contemporary work or a classic – the effect is grand, overwhelming and indelible. No one, I believe, can think of John le Carré's Smiley, for example, without having Alec Guinness firmly in mind.

The understated style he applies to his daily life. His love of concealment is self-evident in his work and personality. His modesty is sincere and unaffected like his acting. He is able to portray enigmatic figures who are mysterious, inward and intense because he himself is all these things. He is also a brilliant comedian and a wonderful raconteur.

There are many stories he likes to tell against himself. Two are illuminating: he claims to have been knighted in 1959, not for his services to the theatre and cinema, but for quelling a riot in Mexico City. It seems the British were rather unpopular in Latin America at the time, and Guinness, a guest at the Mexico Film Festival, made a speech in Spanish which he had learned by heart and which transformed the ugly mood of the natives. The British Prime Minister, Harold Macmillan, showed his gratitude accordingly.

[1] Sir Tyrone Guthrie (1900–71), perhaps the foremost theatre director of his generation.
[2] For a lively account of his war service see *Blessings in Disguise*.

The other story, both in itself and in his telling of it, seems to me to illuminate best Guinness the man and Guinness the actor. One winter's day he entered a grand West End hotel for lunch. The cloakroom attendant took his hat and coat. Guinness asked for a ticket. The attendant said that was unnecessary, smiled and nodded reassuringly. Guinness was rather pleased. The man had obviously recognised him and that made a nice change. After lunch he returned to the cloakroom and the attendant duly handed over the correct hat and coat. As he was leaving the hotel, Guinness reached into the pocket of the coat and found a piece of paper. On it was written, 'Bald with glasses.'

JOHN
GIELGUD

One of the first people to recognise Guinness's talent and, both as actor and director, to exert an important influence on his career, Gielgud (b. 1904) is one of the great performing artists of this century and one of the most loved. He has been at the top of his profession – in the theatre, films, radio and television – for over sixty years and returned to the stage in London last year in Hugh Whitemore's *The Best of Friends*. He was knighted in 1953 and made Companion of Honour in 1977.

EARLIEST STAGES
JOHN GIELGUD

It was way back in 1934 that I was asked to judge an end-of-term performance at the Fay Compton School. Who the other judges were I cannot remember, but I know I had to leave before the awards were officially announced because I had to get back to the theatre, where I was acting at the time, so that on this occasion I didn't meet the winner. I do, however, very vividly remember being greatly struck by the evident talent of a skinny boy with a sad pierrot face and big ears to whom we all agreed the prize should be given.

The plot of the short play in which he appeared was about the owner of a Punch and Judy show who, in despair at losing his customers as they drifted away to some other attraction, went home and, like Mr Punch, battered his wife to death. It seems to me that there was no dialogue, and that the boy's compulsive miming impressed us all very much. A few weeks later I was making up in my dressing room at Wyndham's Theatre when I was told that a young man wished to see me. It was, of course, the young fellow whom we had given the prize to, and he was extremely shy and diffident and refused to accept the few pounds I ventured to offer him. But fortunately I did not forget him, and was able to suggest his being engaged to play Osric in my forthcoming revival of *Hamlet*, which was to open a short time later.

Alec Guinness has often recounted this story, as well as the agonies he suffered during the *Hamlet* rehearsals owing to my

impetuous and somewhat hysterical direction. He afterwards
worked with me, in several minor parts (and, I am sure, for a very
small salary) in *Romeo and Juliet* (as the Apothecary) and *The Seagull*
in which he was only a workman who draws the curtain back for
Konstantin's play in the first act. But I was very pleased to promote
him during my season in 1937–8 at the Queen's Theatre, when he
played Aumerle in *Richard the Second*, Snake in *The School for
Scandal*, the young officer with the camera in *Three Sisters* and
Lorenzo in *The Merchant of Venice*. In all of these plays he gave
excellent performances. He also acted for me in *Noah*,[1] as one
of the animals and he was lucky enough to find another animal
in the cast (Merula Salaman as she was then) whom he was
to marry shortly afterwards and they have been together ever
since.

At this time, although I had the temerity to direct most of these
productions myself, I was also greatly indebted and encouraged
when working under the direction first of Theodore Komisarjevsky and then Michel Saint-Denis, though Tyrone Guthrie (an old
friend from the Oxford Playhouse Company in the early 1920s)
seemed to me rather slapdash and eccentric as the director of my
School for Scandal, and, although fashionably popular already, he
had not yet reached the peak of his brilliantly adventurous career.
He had, however, not failed to remark the great potential ability
of Alec Guinness, and became his mentor and loved friend as well
as giving him magnificent opportunities in classic parts.

In spite of my fondness for him over those merry years, Alec is
not an easy man to know. He has never confided to me his
ambitions, his hopes and his despairs. His sly humour and affectionate nature have always delighted me, as well as making me
very proud to think I had the luck of starting him off on the
wonderful success that was to follow.

We have only worked together once since those early days in
the 1930s – a rather crude duologue by Friedrich Dürrenmatt in
which we were neither of us very happy, and I have never appeared
in a film with him, when I know I should have learnt much by
studying at first hand some of the fascinating mysterious secrets
which have enabled him to create so many different types of
characters with so much subtlety and skill.

I know he loves the theatre as much as I do, and I fancy that he

---

[1] By André Obey (1892–1975), directed by Michel Saint-Denis.

regards it, as I do, as the most valuable basis of his acting, trying to return to it as often as he can.

But not even the most famous and talented screen actors, all over the world, can rival Alec's mystery in acting for the screen or in the theatre, and he never seems to fail in surprising one, in either medium, by his dedicated gift of expressing the thoughts and intentions of whatever part he undertakes to play. On his seventy-fifth birthday I rejoice to congratulate him and embrace him as one of my dearest and most talented of friends.

J.C. TREWIN

Alec Guinness made his debut in the London theatre in *Libel!* at the Playhouse on April 2nd 1934. J. C. Trewin (b. 1908), the doyen of British drama critics, was in the audience. Since then he has seen almost all Guinness's performances and written about a great many of them. Trewin was literary editor of *The Observer* and the paper's second dramatic critic, 1943–53. He was also dramatic critic for *John o'London's*, the *Birmingham Post* and the *Lady*. He is the author of many splendid books about actors, acting and the theatre.

A THINKING MAN

J.C.TREWIN

Though I do remember going to the resolute court-room drama, *Libel!* – and nothing so deserved its exclamation mark – at the Playhouse in London during the spring of 1934, I cannot remember Alec Guinness. Reasonable, perhaps, in the circumstances, but a curious way of beginning to write about an actor I came very soon to admire.

Maybe, even then, Guinness, a youth of twenty (birthday on the first night), was keeping himself in check. Not that in this setting he could really have done otherwise. His part, a junior counsel, had no lines; indeed the only picture of the occasion is of an almost detached wig and gown in the second row of the barristers' seats, established between Joe Mitchenson (from the same drama school) and Mark Dignam. Just in front Leon M. Lion is being vigorously theatrical and things are happening beyond him that were not, I hope, common in an average court.

Being engaged elsewhere, I was sorry to miss events some months later when, possibly with a few more lines, Guinness trebled a Chinese coolie, a French pirate, and a British sailor in a play entitled *Queer Cargo* that barely existed after its opening at the Piccadilly. Still, in the autumn of 1934 one had to consult the programme – of the Gielgud *Hamlet* at what was then the New Theatre – to see the name of the young man playing Osric: a fellow with the puzzled half-smile of somebody conscious of his importance and unable to understand his reception by the Prince. Against the actor's unflamboyant temperament, he was clearly a sad exhibitionist in the world of Elsinore, but he was also, we gathered, an acute judge of fencing. Osric has not always been given his due.

From those days it is not easy to recall what Guinness looked like, and for a time not much would help. He was slightly, rather primly built, precisely voiced in a potentially moving tenor, already examining any part with a surgical delicacy. Facially unremarkable, a player's countenance designed for whatever might turn up – though none would cast him for the equivalent of Meredith's bull that walked the meadows in kingly-flashing coat – he had pale eyes that never at any time ceased to act. Long afterwards he described his Osric, 'wisely not effeminate' said Ivor Brown, as 'a very water-lily.' I can hear yet the carefully-fretted affectation at 'It is very sultry, as 'twere – I cannot tell how.' This maybe was more memorable than the superbly made-up Apothecary in *Romeo and Juliet* (1935). So tense was the argument over an Olivier–Gielgud[1] interchange of Romeo and Mercutio that few people, I imagine, marked the seven lines for that convenient Mantuan chemist worn to the bones by his sharp misery.

Yet much was happening then. It was when Guinness joined the Old Vic company under Tyrone Guthrie, in the early autumn of 1936, that we began to wonder about this young man and his unexaggerated virtuosity: the swooping puff-ball of a courtier, Boyet, whom Guinness disliked; another courtier, Le Beau ('Hereafter, in a better world than this I shall desire more love and knowledge of you'); the amiable emptiness that was William of Arden. Early in 1937 and approaching twenty-three, Guinness passed between Osric and Reynaldo in *Hamlet*, and Aguecheek in *Twelfth Night*, quietly wistful, lank-haired hanger-on who never went over the top as Laurence Olivier's extremely funny Sir Toby, a veteran Skye terrier, was apt to do. Miraculously at 23, he was 'Uncle Exeter' in *Henry V*, gravely dignified warrior and counsellor, here much younger than his King. It is simple now to evoke Reynaldo, a figure that used almost to be forgotten in the theatre, Polonius's trusted servant sent to Paris to keep an eye on Laertes. The old man is particularly dithering and inconclusive, but Guinness's Reynaldo, studying his own silences, listened with

---

[1] In this production Laurence Olivier and John Gielgud alternated the parts of Romeo and Mercutio.

a discreet, hooded smile to his master's haverings and found a calm emphasis for the reply to 'You have me, have you not?' – 'My lord, I have.' It might well have been the actor's response, through life, to any dramatist.

During the summer of 1937 he was both Reynaldo and Osric in the Old Vic company that travelled out to Elsinore. There he opened not in the exposed courtyard of Kronborg but in the ballroom of the Marienlyst Hotel through three hours of driving, steady rain – 'bellropes' said Guthrie – that, externally, smothered the Kattegat. I doubt, after seeing him sixteen or seventeen times at the Vic, whether Olivier played Hamlet better than on this Danish night after visiting journalists had arranged nearly nine hundred small and not too well-balanced gilt chairs. Guthrie left to Olivier the final improvised arrangements, but discovered in the triumph of the occasion his own excitement far ahead, the development of theatre-in-the-round. We did not realise that night that Guinness, on Guthrie's instruction, was entering from the rain-swept beach and through french windows, very wet. (According to Guthrie, 'very dramatic').

In the autumn there was a return to Gielgud for eight months, at the Queen's. Nothing very notable, perhaps, except a double in *Richard II*, Aumerle, and the Groom who makes that final unlikely visit to the imprisoned King. Then at length, in *The Merchant of Venice*, Lorenzo's last act at Belmont was spoken for once with the rapt beauty it needs. A few months later Guinness was back at the Vic where presently – it had to happen – he was himself playing Hamlet, acted now in the 'eternity' text, five hours of it. It had been translated to a more or less Ruritanian setting without any of the flourish of Zenda and Hentzau. Guthrie helped Guinness, the actor said, to find confidence; to be, so to speak, the stillness in the eye of the storm. That was one response to the performance. Another came from Robert Speaight, who had been an Old Vic Hamlet in the reign of Harcourt Williams: 'Sensitive and *intimate*, sparing spectacular effect.' I would have added the comment of an old Cornish farm-neighbour of mine in quite another context, 'A thinking man.' No glint of the stagier bravura; Guinness appeared, as always, to be creating a character as he moved, without previous calculation. Possibly this is why some people, looking back, recall more than anything else the group of wet umbrellas and dripping mackintoshes at Ophelia's funeral: Guthrie remembering Elsinore. At this remove I can call up the Hamlet in words that C. E.

Montague[1] used once for Matthew Arnold: 'Lit with the softened light of an imagination more tender and brooding than fiery . . . twinkling with quiet ironies.'

Guinness would follow Hamlet by probably the most under-played Bob Acres in the history of *The Rivals*. Next spring (1939) he was touring with the Old Vic company in Europe and Egypt, gathering together for an impressive list Hamlet, Acres, Chorus (replacing Marius Goring) in *Henry V*, and surprisingly a principal part in *Libel!*, a drama which I doubt he had ever expected to meet again since his hours as a junior counsel. War lowered and broke. For five years, from 1941, he was in the Navy where he was commissioned during 1942 and became commander of an LCIL, otherwise Landing Craft Infantry (Large).

His first part on returning to the London stage (1946) was in his own version of *The Brothers Karamazov* at Hammersmith which had in the cast such challenging actors as Frederick Valk[2] and Ernest Milton[3] (whose haunting and haunted Hamlet Guinness had warmly admired). He went on to *Huis Clos* at the Arts Theatre Club, also a Peter Brook production, set in Jean-Paul Sartre's idea of Hell, a small room where the condemned tortured each other by mere proximity. Thence back to the Vic, to its famous company that was glorifying the New Theatre and from which I think especially of four parts – though two of the others were Shaw's Dauphin and, from Russia, the bogus government inspector. Beyond all else I go to the Fool in Olivier's *Lear* of 1946, never lost among a whirligig of whimsy; neither prancing jester nor piping grotesque, Guinness restored him to his proper place, wry, quiet, true, with a dog's devotion; when at last he slipped from the play we felt for a moment that the candle was out and we were left darkling. Then (1947) the shyly, anxiously credulous tobacconist, Abel Drugger, in Jonson's *The Alchemist*, a recreation that showed how a small part once acted by Garrick could be stroked back into

[1] Charles Edward Montague (1867–1928), dramatic critic, on the staff of the *Manchester Guardian* for nearly forty years, novelist and man of letters.
[2] Frederick Valk (1895–1956). Physically impressive German actor of immense power. Fled from Germany to Czechoslovakia in 1932; arrived in England in 1939.
[3] Ernest Milton (1890–1974). American-born actor who first appeared in London in 1914. Frail, with a spidery gait and a beautiful, but extravagant voice on and off stage.

eager life. Richard the Second, proud weakling, with less pathos than we had hoped and rather less music, has lingered with me for the way in which by touching the sapling-pillars of the set as he moved rapidly round them, Guinness immediately flashed up the dungeon at Pomfret.

In my memory now one of the most exciting things he did, yet I suppose one of the least remarked, was Menenius Agrippa in *Coriolanus*. He was not a natural choice for 'the humorous patrician . . . one that loves a cup of hot wine with not a drop of allaying Tiber in it.' But his speech reminded me, as so often, of a crystal and 'a very opal': we responded to the heartbreak in his voice when he had left the inflexible Coriolanus in the Volscian camp. 'A noble fellow, I warrant you,' says a guard as the defeated patrician moves away. Noble indeed, and never played as a 'character,' mouthing and rubious. At the première, when he stepped upon the stage of the New Theatre, the actor was simply Menenius Agrippa, and there an end.

He would have a score of stage parts in London and North America between this and 1988, a surprise for historians who have decided that Guinness belonged to the cinema. His work covered the arc between high tragedy and the most feather-pated farce. (He was, too, Dylan Thomas in New York: though I wish I could imagine that; somehow I cannot.) Cataloguing is troublesome: still, memory prompts the occasions that first declare themselves. Thus at Edinburgh in 1949, on the path to Broadway, there would be Eliot's Unidentified Guest, Sir Henry Harcourt-Reilly, in *The Cocktail Party*, a play on two levels, metaphysical debate and drawing-room comedy, that found itself, at that early period, in the heart of a sustained critical argument. Guinness, more than any actor we have known, was able, in Sir Henry's words, to work out his salvation with diligence, though the piece itself resisted many writers.

Later, during his return to the West End among the crowded skirmishing of the Festival of Britain in 1951, he appeared again as Hamlet, now on the so familiar stage of the New. Afterwards he would speak of this as a disaster, but four decades have blurred the troubles of a première when the lighting plot went intensively wrong and Guinness's own performance suffered from his burden of responsibility as both actor and, with Frank Hauser, as director. It was a rebellious revival for the period: he was in rebellion against the use of a clutter of rostrums, saying that he saw no reason for making God's gift to the actor, a flat, square stage, into something like the entrance to the Athenaeum. Very well; but on the night fortune defied him, and some of his cast into the bargain. It was long ago; in recollection more does return of a performance during which Hamlet, after thirteen years, had grown in the actor's mind. Sadly, the night shook his confidence, though the small world of the stage had practically forgotten the event when he came back after twelve months in a mild American comedy, *Under the Sycamore Tree*. There he appeared as an Ant Scientist who complicated life by a dive into psychiatry. Not a very good piece, but Guinness had a Midas-touch with the poorest line.

When Guthrie inaugurated the Shakespeare Festival at Stratford, Ontario, in 1953, Guinness chose to play Richard III – I can only just guess at it – and the wistful King of France in *All's Well That Ends Well*. Back in England he seemed – though it may not be anything he noticed – to test his versatility by acting across the decades a run of parts that never halted in a rut, but took in its course, for example, the mock-Mum of *Wise Child*, Simon Gray's bitumen-black 'drag' comedy in which he was immensely genteel in fur coat, blue costume and parted grey wig, his voice squeezed, minced, and intermittently a gruff baritone. He went on to the ferocity and laceration of Jonathan Swift in *Yahoo* which he had devised with Alan Strachan. There was so much else: no resemblance between the Cardinal of Bridget Boland's *The Prisoner*, who has gauze after gauze stripped from his mind during his ordeal in a Continental prison, and the demi-semi-quavers of a blend of starling and marmoset in a French farce, *Hotel Paradiso*. It was far from all he had done on the stage when he explained in effect and persuasively: 'They have very good hot-water bottles at this hotel; I usually call in for one when I'm passing.' The confidence, spoken with Guinness's gentle comic majesty, has endured for me with the *cri de coeur* (much relished, I remember, by Ben Travers) of Pinero's schoolmistress: 'It is embarrassing to break a bust in the house of comparative strangers.'

Guinness, who by now had been knighted, fitted exactly the title-role of Terence Rattigan's *Ross* (1960), man of multiple contradictions, a histrionic introvert. Scene by scene, he established the assurance, the bitterness, the remote quality, everything that composed the T. E. Lawrence enigma. All was well there. Not so in his Royal Court performance of Macbeth (1966), doomed to a setting of bleak, brownish-papered walls under a glaring light, and with a perversely-cast Simone Signoret as Lady Macbeth. That said, his performance, subtly graded and rightly onomatopoeic, had a mounting power that caused one to regret its surroundings. Two years afterwards he was back with the hieratic Harcourt-Reilly and the linked levels of *The Cocktail Party*, 'eternal and evanescent'. This was in his own production at Wyndham's. During the third act, after being accustomed to the metronomic beat of the verse, we were startled suddenly by the grave, quiet delivery of Shelley's lines from *Prometheus Unbound*:

> Ere Babylon was dust,
> The magus Zoroaster, my dead child,
> Met his own image walking in the garden.
> That apparition, sole of men, he saw.

Emotion in the theatre that night was profound.

So forward, through the kaleidoscope that is Guinness, to Julian Mitchell's version of an Ivy Compton-Burnett novel, *A Family and a Fortune*, where no one better captured the essential style, the rhythmic formality; Alan Bennett's *The Old Country* about an English intellectual who has defected to Russia; and, most remarkably, a Shylock in a Chichester *Merchant of Venice* that lived, and lives, because it neglected the clichés of tradition. Nothing florid, though doubtless it would have been foolish to have expected it; we heard and watched a player so identified with his part that the lightest shift of tone was enough to take us to his inmost thought. The man had a natural dignity. We knew also that, if moved, as he was intolerably, by the loss of Jessica, he would be unforgiving. It was some time since any Antonio in that strangely ordered 'strict court of Venice' had had a foe so implacable as this Shylock, setting a face of stone against any attempt to reason with him. Even if we knew the case was already lost, we could not withhold dismay when he listened for a moment to Antonio's heartbeat before Portia's restraining cry. Suddenly, too, it seemed affecting that the Duke, Portia and the rest were so engaged among themselves that they hardly noticed Shylock was leaving the court. When he did it was without the smallest theatrical parade. Those words must speak for Alec Guinness through his stage career. Certainly they do for his Russian diplomatist in an American play, *A Walk in the Woods* (Comedy Theatre, 1988), a performance during which every twitch of the mouth, every half-glance, had to be important.

How many times in this essay have I used the word 'quiet'? 'In quietness and in confidence,' said the prophet Isaiah, 'shall be your strength.' It is Alec Guinness's strength now and always, the strength of a thinking man.

PEGGY
ASHCROFT

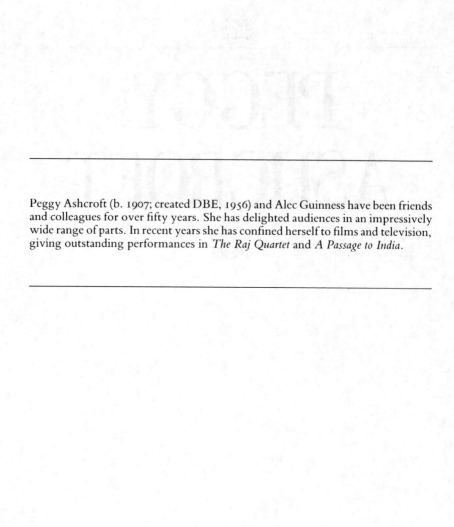

Peggy Ashcroft (b. 1907; created DBE, 1956) and Alec Guinness have been friends and colleagues for over fifty years. She has delighted audiences in an impressively wide range of parts. In recent years she has confined herself to films and television, giving outstanding performances in *The Raj Quartet* and *A Passage to India*.

EARLY AND LATE
PEGGY ASHCROFT

Monday, June 20th, 1988 seems a good day on which to attempt a tribute to my dear friend Alec Guinness for his seventy-fifth birthday next year, as to-day we are celebrating the Golden Wedding of Alec and beloved Merula. It reminds me of how long ago our friendship began.

It was, in fact, fifty-three years ago that I first met him in John Gielgud's 1935 production of *Romeo and Juliet* at the New Theatre, when he played the Apothecary. I look back to that performance and to our last appearance together in *A Passage to India* when he played another mysterious character, Professor Godbole. And I think, if I were to choose a quality to apply fairly uniformly to Alec, it would be MYSTERY – MYSTERY and MISCHIEF. I can still see that rather frightening face peering out at Romeo in Act V – 'Who calls?' A make-up that prefigured that of Fagin which was to appear on our screens not so many years later. Then – 1937 – there was the sly mischief of Snake in *The School for Scandal*, the grave Italian look of Lorenzo in *The Merchant of Venice* – and the ingenuous youth of his Lieutenant in *The Three Sisters* – all at the Queen's Theatre. These were all Early Days, but they remain vividly in my mind after the many memorable masks he has assumed in celluloid.

I jump about fifty years to India – and Bangalore[1]. Only some

[1] For the filming of *A Passage to India* (1984), based on E. M. Forster's novel; directed by David Lean.

of the mystery of Godbole was revealed in the final version – there was an evening when he danced on an enormous stone circle (of perilous narrowness) clashing cymbals of over four feet circumference. The dance was partly rehearsed, partly extemporised, it lasted well over any expected limit, and when finally 'Cut!' brought it to an end, the Indian 'crowd' of some hundreds, who had watched breathlessly, burst into applause. Alas that it was lost in the cutting room. His wit and spirits revived our drooping ones in Bangalore after a long and very hot stint.

That he and 'Merry', as she was called then, shared my house for some time in the later 1930s, after their wedding in 1938 and that we were together for the declaration of war are happy recollections. His extraordinary talent – 'extra-ordinary' – is something that doesn't need me to comment on. His generosity of spirit, his unfailing courtesy and consideration for every member of a company, or film unit, are, perhaps, qualities not so well known. And then – his ability to 'corpse' anyone and everyone as a raconteur of fantastic range – *and* invention!

Dear Alec – faithful friend and most admired colleague, giver of so much refreshment, pleasure and fun – I wish you a Happy Birthday and continuation of friendship and work.

CYRIL
CUSACK

Of all contemporary actors Cyril Cusack (b. 1910) shares an acting style most in common with Alec Guinness. Both favour understatement and both have an unfailing instinct for the truthfulness of a character. Dr Cusack (he received an LLD, *honoris causa*, from the National University of Ireland in 1977) has played everything from Shakespeare and Shaw to O'Casey and Beckett. He has appeared in many television plays and his films include *Odd Man Out*, *The Spy Who Came in from the Cold* and *The Day of the Jackal*. If Ireland were to imitate the Japanese custom, then surely Dr Cusack would be designated a 'National Treasure'.

THE PRESENCE OF ALEC GUINNESS
CYRIL CUSACK

In that rumbling month of August, 1939, said West End impresario, Hugh Beaumont,[1] having gathered me avuncularly towards the cream of English theatre – if only on to the rim of the saucer: 'On no account must you let him know that you are under thirty!' It was something of a cheat.

Making my entrance into words on Alec Guinness I must apologise that I begin so – with myself. But it seems inevitable, I find no alternative; and, after all, are we not actors? And actors understand.

Thus was I introduced into that global company of actors readying for rehearsal of *The Cherry Orchard*, grouped in no particular order on the stage of the Globe Theatre, a music of morning voices. The legendary Michel Saint-Denis would be directing, from whom, in my role of Firs, the old retainer, I must keep dark my years. By himself, in a niche of quiet apart, stood Alec Guinness, as though waiting.

So often dressing-room gossip sends up the cry – 'But it seems only like yesterday!'; and this my first glimpse of the young Alec returns to me now as of just one such yesterday. Is it not true that for some our yesterdays may come alive, resurrected, tumbling mystically into the present? Alec Guinness remains, for me, essentially unchanged from that quietly persistent presence of that yesterday a full half-century ago.

[1] Hugh 'Binkie' Beaumont (1908–73), leading West End impresario; managing director H. M. Tennent Ltd.

This is not to say that what was discernible then as something unique sprung from a seedling of theatrical power would remain static. On the contrary, under the guidance of what I dare to name the 'angelic ego', this actor would proceed gracefully into a continuum of blossomings and flowerings, even through uncertain springtimes; for what player's pilgrimage is free from assailing winds, where the artist for whom there can be growth without pain?

I knew, of course, that sunny morning, who it was, the figure seemingly remote, distant but never dim, to one side of a dazzling roundabout of stage personality, this quiet presence somehow prevailing amidst a late summer storm of genius. The Guinness name, often with the prefix 'Mac' – originally Mac Aonghusa, Son of Aonghus, God of the Birds – suggested I might, myself fresh from the Green Isle, catch a shade of green in the oasis. For the moment bypassing *The Cherry Orchard*, I sidled over to address the lofty patronymic, for it is one that ranks high amongst the lords of the North. It was no mirage. Diffidently, Mr Guinness admitted there might be an ancestral shade or two hovering, however mistily, amidst the hills of Donegal. I was comforted.

I took stock. Peggy Ashcroft was looking with a puzzled air in my direction. She turned and whispered to Gwen Ffrangcon-Davies.[1] 'Look at his face!', I thought I heard. Guiltily I set to examining my script. There was Ralph Richardson, seemingly engrossed in a world elsewhere, happily mispronouncing the Russian names; Saint-Denis calling up from the stalls, 'No, Miss Evans,[2] Madame Ranyevskaia does not cry there!' I clung to the presence of the slim form of the student Trofimov – Mr Guinness – standing by, as telling in his silence as in his utterances . . . one of an array of future titled ladies and gentlemen of the theatre.

The true actor, potentially, is Everyman, which is to identify with everybody, never in mere mimicry, not simply in physical versatility – a curse rather than a blessing, Irish actor F. J. McCormick once said – but in his capacity to reflect the myriad aspects of the wayward spirit of man. So well I might say that, in Guinness the actor, I saw, in some part, myself, recognised my Familiar; despite the rarity of meeting, he had, from the immediacies of our profession, become an intimate.

[1] Gwen Ffrangcon-Davies (b. 1891), distinguished English actress, famed for her Juliet.
[2] Dame Edith Evans (1888–1976), the leading actress of her generation.

It is a truism to say that man is capable of both vice and virtue; it is true to say that the real actor is aware, most deeply aware of these elements at war in our humanity; and Guinness, real actor that he is, resolutely and with increasing power, yet with humble eye set towards a heavenly star, has trod this dangerous pilgrim path to where artistic fulfilment ever waits.

Whether in theatrical or non-theatrical garb and make-up, contained in this actor is a wide assortment of human ingredients that force open the sometimes rusted gate to our affections. We find together the dove and the serpent (New Testament version), innocence and necessary guile; the child within kept whole, protected from worldly invasion, its intuitive wisdom responding selectively to light and darkness, but, alongside, a sharp intelligence with weaponry in readiness for the rude invader; we find in the good Sir Alec a generosity of spirit that sends him hurrying to solace the ageing actress, to comfort the disabled priest; at the same time, let him beware who might, inviting that slow sidelong investigative look, the wasp that can buzz off the tongue with a salutary sting for the pretentious.

What many a good Catholic might say, paradoxically it is next to impossible for a good Catholic to be a good Catholic – yet somewhere amid the elaborate Guinness scenery lurks a spiritual watchman, somewhere a brand of Catholicism – ensconced perhaps in that far ancestry – that was to flare through the portals of the Farm Street church. Whatever the source, with that other convert, his professional ally, Graham Greene, his Catholicism shares a mutuality of Englishness, yet in his film creation of Greene's simple mystic, *Monsignor Quixote*, Guinness reaches a quality of inspiration strangely less English with a kind of holy madness, a fiercely angelic possession as he consecrates the invisible Host.

But Sir Alec can cock an ear to the Rabelaisian, can tell a tale – well distanced, however, from the merely vulgar. And where's the contradiction when, in these days of loose language, on a lapse of concentration he could utter in muffled pain . . . 'Oh, crumbs!'?

Guinness emerging from a Curzon cinema: 'Dickens,' he mutters to himself, blinking into the outlight, '. . . is the greatest!'

I flick over the scattered leafage of the years, quickly skipping past an interim radio relationship in King Lear, and find us at last locked in truly professional brotherhood, not only in the tradition of the stage but as William and Frederick Dorrit in the Dickens classic . . . Dickens, 'the greatest'. And was it not Ronald Knox who described ours 'the most brotherly and sisterly profession in the world', a top-grading to be proud of?

But there may be feudal murmurings in the stage-family too. At Chichester, after watching his magisterial portrayal of Shylock, I went backstage for exchange of fraternal greeting and recall, reminiscence brimful of that pre-war production of *The Cherry Orchard* fated never to reach the gods but condemned to Limbo at the first off-stage roar of Mars. As I was leaving, Sir Alec, still shedding the Shylock beard, poked his head out the dressing-room door and, with a benign smile, called after me, 'I'm never jealous of a good actor.' – a *vale* that should pass echoing down the corridors of theatre. Needless to say, in my vanity I took it for a compliment.

In the end as it was in the beginning, so I conclude – *mea culpa*, with myself. (Anyway, actors do understand, we know the old joke.) But no, wait – not quite – let me rather conclude otherwise: the Guinness presence . . . it persists, lingering through the years, an inspiration to the profession. Here is one who is himself as well as being many others, already leaving a bountiful inheritance to theatre.

The cover of John Russell Taylor's pictorial biography shows an Angus McBean photograph of Alec Guinness, his arms held towards us in an attitude of giving. It describes the true actor's offering – himself.

MERIEL
FORBES

Meriel Forbes (b. 1913), known to her friends as 'Mu', is an actress of beauty and style. Her father was Frank Forbes-Robertson under whose aegis, in 1931, she made her debut in York. In 1944 she married Ralph Richardson (1902–1983).

CHUMS
MERIEL FORBES

Talking on the telephone with Alec is like sitting on a park bench with a very dear chum on a fine day, and time on our hands.

Discussions are lengthy, languid and far reaching. He is invariably acutely funny somewhere along the line, and I (fingers crossed) have never put back the receiver without renewed spirits and fresh happiness.

Alec Guinness, aged 13

Wolf in *Noah* (1935) – an early
example of his talent for disguise.
But which one is he?

As Herbert Pocket in the film of *Great Expectations* with Finlay Currie and John Mills, 1946.

Facing page

As Sir Andrew Aguecheek in *Twelfth Night* with Jessica Tandy and Laurence Olivier, Old Vic, 1936-37.

The Ascent of F6, Alec Guinness (left), Frederick Peisley, Arthur Macrae and Ernest Hare, 1939.

Oliver Twist, Fagin, with John Howard Davies as Oliver, 1948.

Fool in *King Lear,* Old Vic, at the New Theatre, 1946-47.

The Dauphin in *Saint Joan*, Old Vic, at the New Theatre,
1947-48.

All the d'Ascoyne family in *Kind Hearts and Coronets*, 1949.

As Lady Agatha d'Ascoyne

C42·62

Professor Marcus in *The
Ladykillers*, 1955

Gully Jimson in *The Horse's
Mouth* with Arthur Macrae,
1958.

In his Academy Award winning role of Colonel Nicholson
in *The Bridge on the River Kwai*, 1957.

GARRY
O'CONNOR

After Cambridge Garry O'Connor (b. 1942) directed Ben Jonson's *Catiline* at the R.S.C. Stratford studio, *The Keyhole* at the Aldwych, and the London première of Alun Owen's *A Little Winter Love*. He began writing full-time for the *Financial Times* and has since concentrated on plays and biographies. His books include *Ralph Richardson: An Actor's Life* (1982); *Olivier: In Celebration*, which he edited (1987); and the highly acclaimed *Sean O'Casey: A Life* (1988). His *Darlings of the Gods* (1984) has been filmed as a mini-series in Australia, and is due to be shown in 1989.

THE GOOD CAUSE OF CHEERING US ALL UP
GARRY O'CONNOR

Guinness once had a unique way of measuring a performance during the making of a film. His stand-in would come over to him after he had rehearsed a scene and say, 'I loved the way you did that, Alec.' What a sweet and generous comment, Guinness would respond, but then an instinct would tell him, 'Oh, no, that was noticed, it must come out.' Guinness came to rely a great deal on that stand-in for, when he praised something, Guinness knew at once it needed to be removed.

It had not always been so. When he played Herbert Pocket, the pale young gentleman in his first film, *Great Expectations*, in 1946, his ears were pointed, his eyes shone with eagerness, his mouth curled up at the corners. He was repeating an exhilarating stage role. At one point during filming when he had to laugh uproariously he felt he was being exaggerated. The director, David Lean, persuaded him to rehearse quietly and cheated by setting the cameras rolling during the rehearsal.

Guinness wanted so much to play more Dickens he asked Lean out to dinner to try to convince him that he should act Fagin in *Oliver Twist*, Lean's next film. It was the only time in his life, he said later, that he wined and dined a director with a specific part in view. Lean, unconvinced, made him audition and do a screen test. The impersonation which finally emerged in the film was masterly. Basing the old Jew's appearance on George Cruikshank's drawings Guinness brought to his harsh, rasping utterances a pantomime gentleness of movement, while the apocalyptic mood of Lean's direction was powerfully underlined by Arnold Bax's score. But the exaggerated traits of character were still enough to provoke accusations that his portrayal was anti-semitic. Then, as much later, Guinness never minded thoroughly evil people, whom he found more interesting to act than good ones.

Lean taught him to perform the same action identically from take to take. Being neat and liking precision he found that Lean reinforced his taste for understatement and simplicity. Lean steered him through the new world of the cinema – he had just spent five years in the navy – and turned him from grimacing his way through a role to rely on thinking.

Kind Hearts and Coronets brought Guinness hitherto undreamt of acclaim, but a new complication: fragmentation of character into multiple impersonation. Or, as he put it, 'False noses are too easy.' Essentially, in eight speaking parts, one non-speaking part and a portrait in oils – all members of the d'Ascoyne family whom Dennis Price as Louis sets out to murder – he is showing different aspects of the same physical and mental constitution. But true psychological complexity remains with the murderer. Although *Kind Hearts and Coronets* established Guinness as the most gifted character actor in England, he dismissed all these roles as thin stuff – 'Pretty cardboard'. What happened in the darkness after each d'Ascoyne snuffed it – the mysterious limbo in which Guinness would transform himself into something quite new – had become much more intriguing. Who really was he?

This did not become evident in *The Lavender Hill Mob*, for which, he told Edith Evans to her utter amazement, he was paid £6000. His bowler-hatted clerk does have an element of the commanding absence he manages to place at the centre of some of his best film performances, but Guinness is not nearly as interesting in this as he is in *Last Holiday*, in which he showed first his extraordinary capacity for ordinariness. J. B. Priestley's characteristic but wayward script tries to draw a social message out of a man dying of an incurable disease and stops *Last Holiday* from being the more interesting film it might have become had the story been developed more subtly. As George Bird, Guinness, in double-breasted pin-stripe suit and under sentence of death from 'Lempington's Disease', attempts to enjoy his last weeks in a high-class, seaside hotel. Unaffected in every way by the illness, he withholds his secret from the women and other characters to whom he becomes attached, and gains the power, love, and social distinction he previously could never enjoy. Self-doomed to anonymity, Guinness in solitude gains magnetic power. For the first time he shows an ability to convert the screen into an intimate, private means of communication – as if he is revealing something special to each viewer. But he still watches and withholds.

Bird finds out the diagnosis is mistaken, but dies anyway – in a car crash on the day of his reprieve. Guinness's next important role, that of Sidney Stratton in *The Man in the White Suit*, has a similar element of hopes awoken then shattered. In this film Guinness portrays his first man of genius, a scientist who invents an artificial fibre of such impossibly perfect qualities that it threatens the livelihood of millions of textile workers. When the invention causes strikes and an alliance between workers and capitalists the story deteriorates into hysteria, but Guinness's innocent and blinkered quality makes Stratton glow from within and spreads a rich comic sympathy. Again Guinness spends much of the time trying to hide either himself or his clandestine research from the rest of the characters. Privacy and a quality of mind are at the core of his attraction – although the overall effect is in a more Buster Keaton vein.

In *The Card*, the film version by Eric Ambler of Arnold Bennett's novel, Guinness plays another comic upstart, Edward Denry Machin, who rises from humble obscurity to become Lord Mayor in a provincial town. Some have attributed this choice of role to a desire in Guinness to win audiences outside London – he never did the customary stint in an out-of-town touring or repertory company. Others claim that Machin, a man who sets out to conquer the world, presented the challenge of a new kind of hero. Certainly the parvenu capitalist is a most unlikely role: Guinness invests him with tantalising ambiguity, so it is never clear if Machin's actions are above board, or if he is going to be caught as he charms his way into wealth and prominence. 'What great cause has he ever been identified with?' sneers a political opponent on the eve of his adoption as Mayor. 'I think I can tell you,' retaliates the Countess of Choll. 'He's identified with the good cause of cheering us all up.'

Guinness made *Father Brown*, his next film with Robert Hamer, director of *Kind Hearts and Coronets*, seem like a firm return to the circumference of character acting. 'In Father Brown,' wrote G. K. Chesterton, 'it was the chief feature to be featureless. The point of him was to appear pointless; and one might say that his conspicuous quality was not being conspicuous.' It sounded ideal casting, and indeed was, although, paradoxically – and allowing Guinness gives a finely rounded comic performance – he does not achieve invisibility so well as he does with later roles such as John le Carré's Smiley.

He confessed himself dissatisfied and one can see why. Although Father Brown is horrified by the secret and shameful knowledge that every one of us is capable of crime, Guinness's portrayal remains a matter of harmless externals, and he is always owlishly visible. He fails to penetrate the man more than superficially. Guinness was not yet ready to take up full residence in the spiritual centre of a role. But he was wrong to blame himself for not achieving the complete stature of Chesterton's conception: this was probably the fault of the director and other elements in the film, such as the semi-farcical script.

No such impediment held him back as the Cardinal in *The Prisoner*, Peter Glenville's film from the Bridget Boland play in which Guinness had first appeared on stage. In this fictional re-creation of the Mindszenty trial the interrogator, played by Jack Hawkins, peels away the priest's layers of defence not so much by tormenting his flesh as by undermining his sensitivity and revealing the impure motives for his vocation. Some triggers of the guilt are not entirely convincing, but the film quickly reaches a tragic dimension it never loses.

In *The Prisoner* Guinness places before us the naked soul of a prince of the church driven increasingly to desperation: 'I wanted to justify myself to myself. . . To me – not to God . . . I succeeded. I can serve . . . But I can't care.' Playing without hairpiece or other form of disguise Guinness sacrifices neither ordinariness nor humbleness, and suggests depth and greatness. 'Try not to judge the priesthood by the priest,' he tells the young prison guard after his humiliation, echoing St Peter's denial of his master before the cock crows three times.

In *The Prisoner* Guinness finally eschews sentimentality and embraces simplicity. The acting is quite inimitable, for nothing spare, nothing excessive, gives away the actor. 'I wouldn't,' he said later, 'go to a psychoanalyst in case he revealed something and said, "And that is the springboard for such talent as you have."'

I would feel it was just that, was it, instead of having something almost magical . . . like an empathy with animals, something you can't explain, something tucked away inside.' In *Blessings in Disguise* Guinness quotes Teilhard de Chardin, 'The incommunicable part of us is the pasture of God', adding 'I must leave it at that.' It was in the year after playing the Cardinal that Guinness himself became a convert to Roman Catholicism. Peter Glenville acted as his sponsor.

Guinness had never been very happy with the idea, as projected in the Ealing comedies, of himself as the master of a hundred disguises. His last foray into this kind of film was as the buck-toothed and macabre Professor Marcus in *The Ladykillers*, the criminal mastermind whom he endows with eccentricities both disconcerting and reassuring – kindness, intellectual scrupulousness, are as much part of the comedy as the terrifyingly enlarged teeth.

In the nature of this film, Guinness's considerable subtlety of performance is allowed to pass unnoticed: the story itself has an almost perfect symmetry. Otherwise little demand is made on Guinness to extend himself more than he had in *Kind Hearts and Coronets*. But he had more than repaid the Ealing studios for their careful nurturing of his comic gift. The next script from Hollywood that landed through his letterbox – with the accompanying recommendation that it was 'tailor-made for him' – he would return with the sharp observation that, 'no-one has been to take the measurements'. The period of heavy disguises was over – more or less.

So little was his next film made to measure that he had been far from first choice for the part the producer, Sam Spiegel, offered him, and tried to turn it down three times before he finally accepted. Colonel Nicholson had been offered first to Charles Laughton. Noël Coward later regretted turning the part down. Guinness knew Lean did not particularly want him, and he never felt happy during the filming.

If Lean had intended to say that the military ethos on both sides in *The Bridge on the River Kwai*, the Japanese and the British, was equally mad, Guinness tilted the film's sympathies strongly towards Nicholson and traditional British grit and obstinacy. Nicholson is blinkered and humourless; in not allowing his officers to work on the construction of the bridge alongside their men he upholds the letter of international law. But in his refusal to be broken Guinness suggests limitless inner strength and broadens the conflict.

Sometimes his slightly shifty eyes cloud with unspoken emotion; sometimes, after devastated hope, a smiling pride seems to break through pain. Guinness has revealed how he based the half-blind, staggering glide of victory with which Nicholson crosses the parade ground, after his humiliating punishment in the suffocating tin kennel, on the way his son, attacked by poliomyelitis, used to walk. Elsewhere mastery of expressing hidden feeling irradiates the flat, officer-code dialogue: to lines such as 'You're a fine doctor, Clipton, but you've a lot to learn about the army,' Guinness brings a dimension of Nicholson's whole existence. The Colonel grows out of being an inflexible British officer into the representative of order versus chaos, civilisation versus barbarism, echoing Shakespeare's

> Take but degree away, untune that string,
> And, hark! what discord follows

although Guinness's performance, remaining within the narrow limits of Nicholson's mind and physique, remains the very opposite of Shakespearian.

By now Guinness had achieved the status of an international film star. He won an Oscar for *The Bridge on the River Kwai* as the best film actor of 1957. *Time Magazine* devoted its cover and six pages of text to singing his praises. He had made seventeen films, some of them, according to him, 'pretty lousy', partly due to having 'contracts to fulfil.' He regretted not being his own master: 'It's a great mistake, the frightened thing of seeking security.' He especially disliked that element of having no final control over his own performance – and often seeing something that he had been relying on disappear, so that he would have conceived the whole thing differently had he known.

The Horse's Mouth,[1] for which he wrote the script, gave him more control. This was work of superb integrity: close to the novel, its strengths and faults emerge as being almost the same as the book's. But the comic obstreperousness of the painter Gully Jimson, as played by Guinness, is always predictably the same, while the subversive anarchy of Gully's mind is more appealing

---

[1] Based on the novel by Joyce Cary.

on the page than is the physical expression of his artistic ego in the film. It is also, perhaps, somewhat reductive to one's imagination to view his women – his models – made flesh. As Jimson, Guinness is not wholly convincing: but as character impersonation, with white hair, unshaven stubble, gravelly voice, this remains impressive work.

In *Tunes of Glory*, directed by the same director as that of *The Horse's Mouth*, Ronald Neame, Guinness carries off the role of an unreflective egotist with superb self-assurance. The Acting Commanding Officer 'Jock' Sinclair, he claimed on one occasion, was his favourite film role, and 'perhaps the best thing I've done'. Cast against type – Sinclair's disciplinarian replacement played by John Mills was the role Guinness had first been approached to play – Guinness rises magnificently to the challenge of crushing this stickler for form in a conflict, again, between two sets of military virtue. The duel is to the death, and Sinclair wins. 'Whisky for the gentlemen who like it – and for those that don't, whisky' . . . sums up his easy-going, paternalistic attitude to the battalion. It was, as Guinness said, madness to cast him as a drunken, heavy, boorish Glaswegian up from the ranks; but, 'for all my reticence, now and then I like to take a big breath, and semi-explode'.

Note the 'semi-' judiciously placed before 'explode'. Not much bursting out could be detected in some major roles Guinness played between 1960 and 1970: Prince Feisal in David Lean's *Lawrence of Arabia*, General Yegraf Zhivago in the same director's *Doctor Zhivago* and Major Jones in Carol Reed's *The Comedians*. In these he could be said to be marking time until the more fruitful seventies and eighties when he could again attempt 'something impossible,' something which would 'pull out the best of me.'

The first chance came in *Cromwell*, with the role of the martyred Charles I in an interpretation of history unfairly loaded on Cromwell's side – not a story the director Ken Hughes managed to elevate into greatness. With little help from the script Guinness does manage, with stutter and prancing walk, and the variable shading of a Scots accent, to create a memorable existence of a doomed king who, like Colonel Nicholson, thought it his duty to uphold the law. Charles also has a keen sense of humour – more than can be said for Richard Harris's hoarse-voiced Cromwell – and a touching sense of family feeling.

To play Hitler in *Hitler – The Last Ten Days* Guinness engaged in considerable research, at pains to emphasise that Hitler was not an out-of-space monster but a man whom others loved and who was capable of humour. This film failed for all sorts of reasons other than Guinness's central performance. He depicts the ascetic, evil genius in his gloomy, 'No-Smoking', Berlin bunker before all else as a failed artist with flawed vision – one who sacrificed his vocation to restore law and order to his country. It makes a compelling argument to keep the Arts Council grant as high as possible.

Guinness found that in 'his total concentration, in his reliance both on his eye and his ear' George Lucas, director of *Star Wars*, resembled the young David Lean. 'I remember someone on the set criticising Lucas because of his lack of display and announcing that the film was going to be dull. So I took him aside and said, "Mark my words, this film is going to have distinction".' Although the Tolkienesque role of Obi-Ben Kenobi, the exiled and hooded Jedi who promotes the supernatural value of The Force has been described by Guinness as a secondary one, Kenobi's existence, after he has left the screen, grows to assume almost the importance of Godot in *Waiting for Godot*. Once again Guinness creates an existence and a commanding absence – perhaps not really a character at all.

As George Smiley, too, in the television version of *Tinker, Tailor, Soldier, Spy*, and its sequel *Smiley's People* Guinness has again avoided finding the permanent, comfortable role. He has continued the process of stripping away the inessential, even to the point of fearing he might have gone too far so people might say, 'Where's the performance?' Smiley has to 'be a blank and stay a blank', and never give away to the person he is interrogating what he wants to know. But Guinness still had to be real to himself and think along the right lines – sometimes so much of the acting is submerged that all one sees is a periscope gliding swiftly through dark water.

His most recent films have been *Monsignor Quixote* and *Little Dorrit*. As Graham Greene's yellow-leaved and sere version of the Catholic priest, all Guinness had to do, he claimed, was to listen to the ex-Mayor, played by Leo McKern. As old Dorrit, the magnificently deluded father of the Marshalsea debtors' prison, he has returned in a full circle to the much-loved Dickens with whom he started. But even with Dorrit anonymity remains the key to the mystery. No striking effects; no direct emotional statements; an eavesdropping style easy to overlook; nothing larger than life, nothing, in most conventional senses, actorish: why is he simply not dull? That is his secret.

EILEEN
ATKINS

Eileen Atkins (b. 1934) first appeared with Alec Guinness in *Exit The King* by Ionesco in 1963. They became firm friends and have since appeared together in plays and films. An actress of great intelligence and feeling, Eileen Atkins came to prominence in *The Killing of Sister George* in 1965 and was later acclaimed (by Alec Guinness among others) for her performance as Shaw's *St Joan*. Her films include *Equus* and *The Dresser*.

A DIFFERENT PIN-UP
EILEEN ATKINS

My mother and father always voted Conservative, which, as my mother said, living on a council estate in Tottenham, made them 'different'. Wanting to be different was certainly one of the factors that made me want to be an actress (being a dancer which was what I trained to be would certainly not make me different in Tottenham where everyone wanted to be Shirley Temple or a Tiller girl) and looking back I realise that being 'different' affected most of my youthful decisions.

When my class at school was taken to see *Great Expectations*, I took a fancy to Alec Guinness as Herbert Pocket and decided it would be 'different' to have him as my pin-up under my desk lid. It didn't occur to me to write up for a photograph, and it took weeks to find a suitable one as the movie magazines only seemed to have photographs of him as Fagin in *Oliver Twist*, but at last I found one of him looking rather dapper with a hat and cane (or umbrella?) and stuck it under my desk lid. I loved that picture and I felt extremely superior to the other girls in my class who opened their lids to gaze at Frank Sinatra or Cornel Wilde. I also added Dirk Bogarde and James Mason to the desk lid, but I remained faithful to Alec Guinness and saw all his movies that came my way.

I hardly went to the theatre at all when I was young as my parents only went to the music hall and I could only go whilst at drama school if we were given free seats because a play was doing badly. So it came as quite a shock to me when very early in my

63

career I found myself in a play at the Royal Court Theatre with Alec Guinness. To me he was a film star, I didn't expect him to be in an avant-garde theatre like the Court, that was the world I wanted to be in, it didn't have film stars, it was for dedicated grubby actors who didn't care about money or fame.

The play was *Exit the King* by Ionesco and when George Devine asked me to play the part of Juliette I was thrilled because although small it was a good part and I liked the play, but I could see that some people would see Juliette as old and I wanted to make it clear to George before we started that I would play her my own age. It seemed to me pointless to have an actress in her twenties play sixty when there were plenty of actresses of sixty. He agreed that it could be played any age and he wanted me to play it my own age. So we started rehearsals, which was when I first clapped eyes on my pin-up in the flesh.

The first thing I remember about him was that he was determined not to be treated like a star in any way and made it quite clear that he wanted to be one of 'us' – a group of actors doing a play and certainly the first thing I remember him saying to me as I 'Sir Alec'd' him was, 'Oh do please drop the accolade'.

I was extremely miserable as that first week of rehearsals progressed, as I realised that George *did* want me to play it old and not only did I think it more effective played young (she was a drudge chosen to represent someone who knew nothing of life but hard physical labour and I thought the point would be made more clearly if it was a young woman physically exhausted and with no hope of a better life), but George was asking me to do a funny old walk and clearly wished he'd never cast me and I just became more miserable and stubborn.

On the Friday morning of that first week George took me to one side and said he thought it better if I didn't play the part, would I rehearse through to the end of the day and on Monday he'd find another actress. I said 'fine' and, although hurt, part of me was relieved and I went off for a lonely sausage and chips.

When I came back after lunch Alec was waiting for me and took me to one side; 'George has told me what he said to you this morning. I think he's wrong and I've told him so. I think you're going to be very good indeed – and you're quite right, she should be young. So it's agreed you're not leaving. All right?' I'd been on the defensive since I'd left drama school (I'd needed to be, the blows had come thick and fast!). This gesture of kindness and apparent faith in my talent took me utterly by surprise. Apparently Sir Alec Guinness was on my side. He was the first person in the theatre I had total trust in and I've trusted him ever since.

I think I've learnt more about stage craft from him than anyone, which is ironic when I'd thought of him as a film star. In *Exit the King* I was required to wheel him in a wheel-chair for half the evening. It was the first time I was aware of finding the lights on stage because it was my responsibility to get the chair with him in it into the correct position each time. There were also tricky technical things when he had to start to fall and I had to push the chair under him at just the right moment without giving the back of his legs a whack. Alec would rehearse this business meticulously and I found I enjoyed the discipline of getting that chair in exactly the right spot all the time. George rather left me alone and Alec would occasionally, very tentatively, give me a note which I always found to the point and very helpful.

We opened in Edinburgh and apart from the first shock of going to the theatre to find a grey wig waiting for me in my dressing room, which I was evidently supposed to wear and which, instead of just taking it to Jocelyn Herbert, the designer, and George, and saying that I didn't want to wear it, I sprayed it with bright orange hair dye and wore it for the dress rehearsal, after which it was never mentioned again and Jocelyn made me a beautiful turban, I was also very miserable in my digs which were dirty and un-pleasant. Graham Crowden, who had gone with me to them and been as appalled as I was must have told Alec how ghastly they were, for the next thing I knew was that Alec had found me a room at the Caledonian, the grand hotel where he was staying. I was grateful but wondered how I was going to pay. I needn't have worried as when I went to pay the bill I was told it had been taken care of.

It was in this company that I became aware that leading members of companies would take the whole company out to dinner – both Alec and Googie Withers did this – and how, to meet socially as well as on the stage made playing together easier.

Every time I have worked with Alec since then he has always meticulously taken every single member of the company and stage-management out to dinner, either together or in small groups. Of course not everyone can afford to do this, but the general principle has stuck with me from his example – get to know the company you're with and it's up to the older leading actors to make sure the younger, less experienced ones are not shy of you. I'm a naturally gregarious person so this was an easy lesson for me, it is only after years of knowing him that I think it is not so easy for Alec as he is naturally reserved (not shy – reserved) and he doesn't tell his life story after the first glass of champagne, as I tend to – he listens.

Exit the King was the beginning of our friendship, although at that time I wouldn't have called it that, I just felt that a very grand actor had been kind to me. But Alec isn't someone who forgets you when the play you're in together finishes. He kept in touch and came to see my work (indeed, he made me feel so easy with him that when I was in Chicago working and won enough money at the ponytrotting races to pay my fare to New York where he was playing in *Dylan* I rang him up there and invited myself for the weekend) and a few years later he asked me to play in *The Cocktail Party* with him, and from that time I would say our friendship developed.

The Cocktail Party was one of the happiest working experiences I've had in the theatre, and I have had a lot of happy experiences.

An odd thing happened before Alec asked me to play Celia Coplestone in this play. I'd been in New York for eight months in Frank Marcus's *The Killing of Sister George* and I dreamed one night that I was doing a play with Alec on a platform surrounded by green fields and we were both dressed in evening dress and speaking verse, but I knew it wasn't Shakespeare, and out of the back of my evening dress I had a huge cock's tail and I said under my breath to Alec while we were performing 'Have you noticed what's sticking out of the back of my dress?' and he said 'Yes, that's perfectly correct.'

One week later I was back in London and had a telephone call from Alec to ask me to play Celia Coplestone in *The Cocktail Party* at Chichester (which of course is surrounded by green fields). I greeted his offer with stunned silence and then told him of my dream. He was not surprised – he'd pre-dreamed himself and I've now done so quite a few times since.

I'd studied T. S. Eliot quite a bit at drama school as one of my teachers there had been mad about his poetry but I'd never performed it before. Alec was directing as well as playing Reilly and the notes that I remember getting from him seem simple now but you'd be surprised how rarely you get really useful help from a director. I remember one rehearsal being frightfully pleased with myself because I'd finally worked out exactly what Eliot meant (and of course the work is very dense and difficult to make clear to audiences) and I thought to myself 'now I made absolute sense of that' and Alec said 'Yes, now you know exactly what you're saying but you're spelling it out to us – because *you* know exactly what you're saying you can now gather it up – the audience will understand.' Oh how often I have sat in audiences since saying to myself 'Yes, yes, don't spell it out to me GATHER IT UP!'

I'm nervous enough of critics but no-one makes me more nervous than Alec. I think it is because he has such high standards (and is more rigorous with himself than anyone – I don't think he's ever been really pleased with any work he himself has done) that you know that you won't get away with anything. He tries to be honest about performances he sees without being unkind, so that in a world of 'You were marvellous, darling' his approbation really means something.

Of course that is the unnerving thing about him socially – you know he's not missing a trick (his own book *Blessings in Disguise* is a wonderful example of that) and when I'm with him I tend to think 'just tell the truth, he'll know if you're being false.' Which is of course the basic rule of a good actor. To be true.

During the Chichester season I often stayed with Alec and his wife Merula (who is one of the few really good people I know who is also huge fun) and had I not been having a very unhappy love affair at the time, which Alec I know must have disapproved but never showed his disapproval, it would have been a lovely summer. (Incidentally when the affair came to a sticky end and I immediately rang Alec and Merula and asked them if I could come and stay for a few days, I couldn't have made a better choice. I knew that they'd be quietly sympathetic but I wouldn't be able to indulge in self-pity and there would be a general feeling that it was a good thing it was over.)

We transferred *The Cocktail Party* first to Wyndham's Theatre, then to the Haymarket. It was very enjoyable apart from a few arguments with Binkie Beaumont who hated my clothes for the play at Chichester and wanted them changed for the London run. It was the time of the mini-skirt and I was supposed to be playing someone fashionable (the idea was that we played in a sort of classical modern dress but of course this is very hard for women, our fashions change so much more radically than men's). Binkie couldn't bear the sight of my knees, I don't think Alec could either but he kept quiet about it, and then, because I lost on the arguments about my knees – they were decently covered – I rebelled about my hair and had an Afro hairstyle. Alec only allowed himself one comment, 'Celia ends up with the natives. I don't think she should look like one at the beginning of the play'.

I'm always deeply suspicious of actors who *never* laugh uncontrollably on stage (or 'corpse' as we call it). It seems to me that if you don't find it funny when someone who is making a very grand speech, trips or has a fly settle on their nose, or you see their flies are undone, or you hear someone snore just when you've been particularly eloquent – then you're lacking a sense of the ludicrous and you will be a rather boring actor. Of course it is bad for the audience to be aware of these lapses unless it's quite obvious to them as well (for example when the chair that you're sitting on collapses beneath you) when I think you might as well share the joke and then get on with the play, but Alec does wickedly funny things on stage to make you laugh.

I was once in his room before the show going on about how attractive Steve McQueen was and how sexy mouths like his were where the upper lip looked almost rolled back (Brigitte Bardot, Jeanne Moreau and Mick Jagger). Just as the curtain rose for the first act, where Alec had his back to the audience and we were all facing him and the audience, we saw that he'd sellotaped his upper lip up. He cleverly whipped it off as he turned round but I had a difficult moment or two controlling my laughter.

Another time I was losing my voice and Alec was a bit irritated with me as he had held that if you produced your voice properly and didn't get too tired you need never lose your voice. Mr Punt, the voice specialist, had been treating me at the theatre before the evening performance and I'd told him Alec was a bit cross, so he left a note in Alec's dressing room saying 'You must not be cross with Miss Atkins, she has difficulties because all her passages are narrow.' That evening when Alec handed me the piece of paper on which he was supposed to write the name of the convent I was to go to, he'd written '*All* your passages narrow?'

But mostly it's the unplanned things that make one lose control and one night we could hardly continue when after Alec had said Reilly's line to Celia about a man she'd had an affair with 'And what does he seem like now to you?' a member of the audience shouted out 'A cunt'. We couldn't believe our ears. We looked at each other's faces and realised we *had* heard it and said afterwards that we'd both had the same image of this poor man who'd been dragged to the theatre by his wife, hadn't understood a word all evening, had had too much to drink in the interval and through the mist of the second half realised that at last he understood the situation.

I've only worked with Alec since on the television film of *Smiley's People*, where we had a month of filming in Paris. Once again I learned something invaluable from him. To my amazement he uses a loud clear voice when filming, a medium where some actors talk so quietly (much more quietly than anyone does in real life) that you can't hear your cues. When I asked him about this he said 'You can colour what you're saying more clearly if you use a full voice and the sound people will turn it down. I find the performance is rather flat if I use very little voice.' I've found this to be absolutely true.

We had great fun in Paris. I hardly knew it and he took me out whenever he had time. He often dressed down and wore a black beret and carried a string bag so that he could walk unmolested round the streets. He manages very well the thing of not being recognised when he doesn't want to be, which is really all the time except in restaurants where he wants good service.

I often wonder what he likes about me as I can talk sensibly about very little except acting, but he has the gift of friendship and he's given it to me along with all the nuggets of truth about acting that he's collected over the years and the fact that he *does* like me means a great deal to me.

FRANCO
ZEFFIRELLI

Distinguished director of opera, plays and films. Born in Florence in 1923, he studied English as a boy and towards the end of World War II acted as interpreter for the Scots Guards. His international reputation was largely made in England with a stunning production of *Romeo and Juliet* at the Old Vic in 1960. His productions of opera are acclaimed throughout the world and his films include *Romeo and Juliet, The Taming of the Shrew, Jesus of Nazareth, La Traviata* and *Brother Sun, Sister Moon* in which Alec Guinness played the part of the Pope.

SURVIVING GIANT
FRANCO ZEFFIRELLI[1]

We often talk about the sad reality of our time and regret the
passing of the giants. Gigantic personalities, in the arts, in all
aspects of life, seem to become fewer every day. Like dinosaurs
they no longer reproduce themselves. Alec Guinness happens to
be one of the very few survivors, an active survivor, of a planet
which was once populated by giants.

I remember distinctly the first time I heard his name. Italy was
occupied, in a state of war and turmoil. But from England came
glimpses of what the world had been, of what it should be again,
the world of art and theatre, great actors and great performances.
I was then in my late teens and had an insatiable longing for
culture. There was talk of a fascinating pre-war[2] production of
Hamlet by Tyrone Guthrie with Alec Guinness. I had to know
more about it. I kept pestering anyone, everyone, asking to be
sent reviews, photographs, articles. I must have been a pain in the
neck. In due course, my persistence paid off because things began
to arrive. The production had been controversial, in modern dress,
with a famous graveyard scene, the mourners sheltering under
shiny black umbrellas and Guinness wearing gumboots. The critics
were particularly startled by the interpretation of the relationship
between Hamlet and his mother. The production entered my
mythology and Alec Guinness ascended Olympus, a giant.

[1] In conversation with the editor.
[2] In 1938.

The first time I visited London the play I most wanted to see was Alec Guinness in *Ross* by Terence Rattigan because it combined two of my great heroes, Guinness and T. E. Lawrence. I saw the play and was overwhelmed. It was wonderful, fantastic, one of the greatest emotional experiences I have ever had in the theatre. I went three times, I think, and stood at the stage-door to catch a glimpse of Guinness as he left the theatre.

I met him for the first time a few years later. He and his wife, Merula, attended a performance at Covent Garden of *Lucia di Lammermoor* which I had directed. They came backstage to congratulate Joan Sutherland and asked to meet me. I was in absolute awe of him, speechless, behaving like an extremely stupid fan. He couldn't have been very impressed with this young Italian who could apparently perform miracles on stage but who, in person, was stammering and stuttering, barely articulate. But he was very kind, incredibly polite, very respectful and attentive.

We shared a great agent, Dennis van Thal, and he kept us in touch with each other and we met occasionally. For example I invited him to see my production of *Romeo and Juliet* at the Old Vic. He came to a matinee for schoolchildren and was absolutely enthralled by their excitement. As you know, he is not a very expansive man. When you meet him and he says something it is as if you have only seen the tip of an iceberg. There seems to be so much unspoken that you have to guess how much he feels and doesn't or can't express.

We have, regretfully, only worked together once when he played Pope Innocent II in the film *Brother Sun, Sister Moon*. He loved doing it. For us it was an extraordinary coup. The other members of the cast were unknown young English actors and here, among them, was this giant. And he was presented as a giant. His first appearance in the film was at the top of a gold-encrusted staircase with gold mosaics, Byzantine, embodying the glory of the Church. He really was the personification of glory. When he descended the long flight of stairs, each step he took was a coming down to earth, as it were. All the glory, the paraphernalia, the accessories fell away. He came down to this group of poor young friars and even in his white robes he really was like God laid bare. He talked to them in a fatherly voice, quite wonderful, tired apparently, but deeply sincere and compassionate. One had the impression he envied them, these young friars, for their simplicity and poverty. There he was trapped in luxury and glory desperately wanting to begin his life again, perhaps on a different course, perhaps to be poor and simple like those young friars. I have a feeling Guinness is a bit like that himself. He doesn't like to talk about his past achievements. He is constantly thinking, or so it seems to me, of what he can still contribute.

He worked for only one week on the film. He came and went. I wish I had seen more of him then and I wish I saw more of him now. He is very withdrawn. We exchange Christmas cards, affectionate greetings, but I don't see him. It's difficult, of course. I come to London infrequently and for very short periods. He lives in the country and so meeting is difficult. He is an elusive personality in every way but why should he be anything else? Why should he be pinned down? You see, it's the tip of the iceberg again. The English would call him shy but I don't think he's really shy. He is, from my point of view, the exact opposite of the Latin temperament. But when you need him, he's there. Why should he be expansive? He is a great artist. He is what he is. I'd love him to come to stay at my villa in Positano, to spend some time there, to talk, so that we could get to know each other better. But I can say this: he is one of the great memorable personalities I have had the privilege of meeting.

IRENE
WORTH

Irene Worth is an American. In 1942 she came to England, studied with Elsie Fogerty and began her career in the English theatre. She is a close friend of Sir Alec Guinness and has played with him in Shakespeare, Eliot and Feydeau. She now lives for most of the year in New York. Her recent appearances at the National Theatre were as Volumnia in *Coriolanus* and as Valentina in *The Bay at Nice* by David Hare.

DEFYING EXPLANATION
IRENE WORTH

How can a man say 'yes' and bring the house down – no signalling to the audience by intonation or gesture that a laugh is on its way, only a steely simplicity and the power of thought?

Alec has natural presence which he has carried from the beginning through hardships and this has supported his genius in spite of his many doubts about his talents. He is an original thinker and very daring. He questions every role he plays with a sharp intelligence. His fearful eye on us, on mankind, leaves no unturned stone unturned. He will use his surreal eye when he can. His realism is not representational. He is never glib. He questions everything.

I think of his reluctance to cut the 'little eyases' speech in *Hamlet*, his combat with Tyrone Guthrie over the amount of ooze on the sack which held Hastings' head in *Richard III*. Sir Tyrone Guthrie asked Alec to come to Stratford, in Canada, and play the leading roles in a new kind of open-stage theatre he was planning. Alec asked me to join him in the chosen plays: *Richard III* and *All's Well That Ends Well*.

I remember the loneliness of his Richard III as he sat, horribly alone, silent, his Coronation train covering the stage, his eyes filled with fear and guilt, his voice, in a rasp, saying, 'I am not in the giving vein today.' I remember his dying, exquisite King in *All's Well*, whom I wheeled about in a wicker bath chair. I hear his gentle voice: '. . . since I nor wax nor honey can bring home, I quickly were dissolved from my hive.'

Alec won't live in the bustle of a city. He and his wonderful wife Merula, their son Matthew not too far away, live in the country and their love and knowledge of nature is strong. There one finds them in their element, without pretension, with their animals, books, paintings, answering the telephone, reading, writing. There are no photographs or paintings of Alec standing about. One might be amazed to discover that he was an actor if one strayed in from an unknown land.

It is not until the text strikes him that his forces sharpen and then he begins the excitement of his ideas. Who can forget those dreadful teeth in *The Ladykillers*, the closing actions of the closet scene in *Hamlet*, the frightful, blood-curdling walk to the murder of Duncan, the flashes of the purest truth in acting during the close-ups of his Smiley.

When we were playing in Feydeau's *Hotel Paradiso*, he made his entrance sharpening a pencil, slicing away at it with his pen-knife until he had nearly walked over the footlights into the laps of the audience. Only then did he become aware that anyone was regarding him. Peter Glenville had directed us to perform with intense speed and earnestness and when Alec had hidden from my husband inside the chimney and returned, quite black with soot, he said, 'It's me, Marcelle,' with such concern and reassurance to me that the audience began to laugh louder than ever. I shouted to him, over the roar, 'Shall I wait or go on?' He shouted back, 'Go on!' We did.

His talent is prodigious. We become impatient to see more roles for him to fill with his talents, imagination, eye, vision – the eye of Cartier-Bresson, of Picasso, of Man Ray.

When I, as Celia, had the good fortune to play the 'break-up of the affair' scene with Robert Flemyng in *The Cocktail Party*, Robert's performance had been so profound that he had prepared the ground for the great 'consulting room scene' to follow. Alec Guinness then said 'Yes', and brought the house down. He was Sir Henry Harcourt-Reilly, having dealt with a wrecked marriage. When the couple left, Alec lay down on his own consulting room couch and put a handkerchief over his face. The telephone rang, he answered it and said, 'yes'. I don't know what alchemy he used. I often watched him from the wings before my entrance. There was nothing to see – only Alec at the telephone and the audience laughing with delight. His brilliance defies explanation.

After the laughter, Alec prepared a stillness for my entrance which made it possible for us to play the ensuing scene sitting, without a move, until it ended perhaps twenty-five minutes later. His stillness allowed Celia to pour out her heart. His stillness was like the stabiliser of a great ship. Alec's love and knowledge of the sea are not wasted. His stillness was like the sea.

SIMON GRAY

In 1968, in his first play, *Wise Child*, Simon Gray (b. 1936) required Alec Guinness to play an ageing thug dressed as a woman. Since then Gray has written some of the most successful and intelligent plays of the last twenty years. The list is long and distinguished and includes *Butley*, *Otherwise Engaged*, *Quartermaine's Terms* and *Melon*. Most recently he directed his own play *The Common Pursuit* both in New York and London. He is also the author of several novels and two brilliant theatrical diaries.

HOLY ORDERS

SIMON GRAY

Before I'd had a chance to read Sir Alec Guinness's memoirs, I'd
have been willing to take bets that neither my name, nor the title
of my first stage play, *Wise Child*, in which Sir Alec played the
lead, would be found in the index. My confidence on this matter
came from experience. I've read many interviews given by Sir
Alec in the last fifteen years or so, and never once found, however
retrospective his mood, any mention of our association. From
which I deduce that though *Wise Child* took up a good (or bad?)
six months of his life, it was, for him, of only fleeting consequence.
For me, of course, it remains a major event.

In the summer of 1966 I was holidaying in Portugal with my
family. One afternoon a telegram arrived from my agent announcing that Michael Codron had sent my first stage play, *Wise Child*,
to Sir Alec, who wanted to meet me at once, with a view to doing
it. So we packed up a week or two earlier than we'd expected or
wanted, and returned in possession, for part of our journey, of a
live chicken, a gift from our landlord, who owned the abattoir in
which we'd taken rooms. I have now reached a stage in my career
when I wouldn't dream of breaking off a holiday[1] merely because
an actor wanted to meet me. This isn't because I've become vainer
– though I probably have – but because I've learnt that actors either
want to do your play or they don't want to do your play, although
they sometimes need to be thought to need to be talked into doing

[1] Even one taken in an abattoir. But that's another story.

your play. But Sir Alec had, I subsequently understood, a particular reason for checking me out. The subject of *Wise Child* – transvestitism, bizarre sexual passions, etc. – was such that he wanted every possible guarantee that the author wasn't himself a freak. So – resisting the temptation to slip into one of my wife's dresses and a pair of her high heels – along I went to his London pied-à-terre, for dinner à deux.

It was, needless to say, an immensely civilised evening, in which we quoted to each other from the poems of T. S. Eliot, he in movingly canonical tones, I with the briskness of a respectably married university lecturer. My nerves, of course, were playing me up in their usual fashion, but I dealt with them pretty effectively in my usual fashion – by drinking steadily. The evening was a total triumph, I felt and still feel, until the moment the door closed behind me, and I tottered down the path, across the pavement, fell into the gutter, was sick. I had an impression that a curtain twitched in the pied-à-terre, and a compassionate face peered towards me through the darkness, but that may have been an illusion. And even if it wasn't, the sight of a respectably married university etcetera rolling drunkenly in the gutter was probably vastly more reassuring than the sight of a departing transvestite would have been, however sober. Anyway, Sir Alec duly signed up, and we were off.

The rehearsals for *Wise Child* were of course the first professional rehearsals I'd ever attended, and I'm glad to remember that Sir Alec and the director, John Dexter, were perfect hosts, offering greetings in the morning when we met, salutations in the evening when we separated, and during the rehearsals themselves finding for me a quite comfortable chair in a far-ish corner of the room from which I could see and hear something of what was going on. The rest of the cast consisted of Gordon Jackson, who played a rapacious, God-intoxicated homosexual; Simon Ward, who played a motherless but mother-fixated homicidal maniac; and Cleo Sylvestre, who played a simple-minded cockney West Indian. The plot, and the violently farcical sexual collisions and corruptions arising from it were too complicated for our then national theatre censor, the Lord Chamberlain, to work out, so he let slip by, and onto the public stage, a play that everybody connected with it enjoyed for its boisterous bad taste. Its *blasphemously* boisterous bad taste.

I spent quite a lot of time with Gordon, Simon and Cleo in a pub around the corner after rehearsals, while Sir Alec and John Dexter spent quite a lot of time together, presumably conferring on matters either artistic or canonical or both. John Dexter at that time – I haven't worked with him since – seemed to me an astonishing combination of the pragmatist and the magician, producing most of the results I'd intended in the writing with a minimum of fuss, although his manner veered between the constantly and calmly reverential when addressing Sir Alec to the crisply abrasive when addressing the other actors. He also knew about this activity called 'blocking', a word the meaning of which I didn't understand at that time, but which awed me. He was small, balding, blue-jowled and stocky, with a ferocious emotional under-current and an intelligence of obvious ferocity. I think I would have admired him without reservation if I hadn't been disturbed by the discrepancy between his manner to Sir Alec and his manner to the other three actors. To me, stranded in my corner and at an awkward angle to the action, he was wonderfully polite, making sure I got my cups of coffee and biscuits, now and then consulting with me about the text, accepting a clarification here, gaining endorsement for a cut there. And in fact, I only had one difficult passage. At the end of the first act my text called upon the character played by Sir Alec, togged up as Simon Ward's surrogate mother, to recoil in disgust from a particularly perverted outburst from the Simon Ward character, and then in spite of him/herself – moved by the Simon Ward character's display of pain (jealousy) – to put an arm around him and cuddle him into comfort, on which image *lights down* and *curtain*. The problem, from my point of view, was that we were getting the disgusted recoil but not the pitying cuddle, so that *lights, curtain* descended on an image of Sir Alec keeping a morally refined distance from the surrogate child I'd wanted him not to be able to withdraw from. I pointed this out to John Dexter who impassively drew me over to Sir Alec and had me point it out to him. Sir Alec listened with seraphic gravity, and then the two of them retired for one of their canonically artistic conferences. After rehearsals John Dexter came over to me as I was about to head for the pub and put it to me that as we were only a few days off our first (of three, I think it was) previews, Sir Alec would prefer me not to attend any further rehearsals, I had an unsettling effect on his quest for the truth of the part. At the first preview, the interval curtain fell on a tableau of a blubbering Simon

Ward, and a Sir Alec Guinness, in his wig, skirt, blouse, etc., in fastidious recoil.

Alas, Sir Alec's noble attempt to purify the ending of the first act went unnoticed by critics and public alike. *Wise Child* was a succès de scandale – granted, that is, that it was a succès d'anything. It ran for the four months Sir Alec was contracted to play in it. His initial affection for the piece was, I suspect, gradually eroded by the reaction of his long-established admirers, who doubtless expected from him, even in his comedies, a touch of the spiritual – failing that, certainly a dash of gentlemanliness. But there was no place for spirituality or gentlemanliness in the character I'd provided for him – an ageing thug who cavorts about in a wig, skirt, high heels, squawking out gross indelicacies while tippling from a concealed bottle of whisky – simultaneously trying to have it off with the Cleo Sylvestre character, while being sucked into a deeply unhealthy relationship with the psychopathic Simon Ward character. At an early performance a gentleman of the old school rose in the middle of the first act, shouting: 'I thought you were above this sort of thing, Sir Alec!'[1] and led his family out, a righteous goose[2] at the head of a dignified gaggle. There was also a great deal of simple incomprehension, especially from Americans, who bought tickets only because they expected to see Sir Alec live. Some of them wondered for nearly two hours, aloud, when he was going to appear, and when he finally, in the closing minutes, ripped off his skirt, blouse and wig, failed to identify him – perhaps because Sir Alec had a short-cropped ginger wig under his middle-aged female wig that made him seem even less like himself than when dressed up as a middle-aged woman. One evening, well into the second act, I heard the following exchange, between two elderly mid-Western (from the sound of them) ladies:

Lady A: 'Hey, that boy' (Simon Ward in a wig, but otherwise passing himself off as a male) 'has he got problems!'
Lady B: 'Yeah, but the mother' (Sir Alec in a wig, passing himself off as a female) 'there's something funny about her, too. If you ask me.'

---

[1] For the producer's version see page 101.
[2] Gander, now I come to think of it.

And Sir Alec's fan letters – if they were anything like the ones I got – must also have had an unsettling effect. I received a number of alarming invitations, though the only one I still remember would have involved my standing under the clock at Waterloo Station at precisely ten minutes to nine p.m. – presumably we were to take a train together, to somewhere unthinkable,[1] some chap and I.

So probably it's not surprising that whenever I dropped in on Sir Alec in the dressing-room on my way home from college, our conversations were somewhat strained. Especially, as I always seemed to catch him in the last stages of preparation – sitting in front of the mirror, in his wig, skirt, blouse and high heels, dabbing on rouge or stroking on lip-stick, his eyes briefly meeting mine in what I came more and more to feel was a kind of reproach. I on the other hand was in my normal togs, my brief-case in my hand, every inch a respectable university et cetera, on my way home to dinner with my wife and child. In retrospect I can also see that it's not surprising that for Sir Alec four months in the part were quite enough. And why I was unlikely to figure in his volume of memoirs, even though it's called *Blessings in Disguise*.

---

[1] Leamington Spa! There, I've thought it.

CORAL
BROWNE

Born in Melbourne, Australia, in 1913, Coral Browne made her London debut in *Lover's Leap* at the Vaudeville in 1934. Since then she has been a leading actress in the theatre – on both sides of the Atlantic – and in films. In 1983 she starred in *An Englishman Abroad* with Alan Bates, based on her own experience of a meeting in Russia with Guy Burgess. She is married to the actor Vincent Price.

A DAY IN THE COUNTRY
CORAL BROWNE

The friendly tap at the bedroom door came at 'about 8.30', as
requested. The rather wonderful routine of a day in the country,
luxuriating in the friendship of Alec and Merula, was beginning.
And, with this polite summons, the perfect host was delivering
breakfast, personally and unobtrusively.

He drew open the curtains. The sunlight flooded in to illumine
the Evian water, the hot toast, butter and bitter marmalade gleam-
ing, the coffee fresh filtered. Not par for the course at the Guinness
household – certainly, the cosseting of breakfast in bed was habitual
– but this was a Coral Browne Price menu, prepared precisely to
her taste, and, probably, by the bearer himself.

He stood a moment in the rich pile of the bedside carpet, the
entire room meticulously furnished and appointed for the comfort
and pleasure of guests. In attending to his friends, Alec is lavishness
itself.

This was the summer of 1982, at his home in Hampshire. Our
friendship had prevailed for more than thirty years, since our first
meeting, after I had sat in awe of his performance as Dr Simpson
in *The Human Touch*.[1]

It was the Guinness touch I was experiencing now. He smiled a
welcome, endearing his presence.

'Lovely morning,' he acknowledged in that voice that can move

[1] By J. Lee Thompson and Dudley Leslie, Savoy Theatre 1949, directed by
Peter Ashmore.

from comedy to tragedy in little more than half a tone and only the slightest pressure on the delivery pedal.

This brief hello and he was gone, the soul of discretion. Discretion is his by-word, both personally and professionally. He rarely invokes the 'I' in his telling observations; the first person is the last to enter his brilliant mind. His autobiography is told only through the involvement with others. A truly formidable, invisible man.

He had employed immaculate timing in delivering the morning meal, bowing out before I could truly appreciate his presence, allowing me to relish breakfast at my own pace and in my own way.

The repast was to me perfection, and I surmised that, in the house below, Merula was bustling over domestic affairs, possibly out with the dogs, or tending the goats or flowers and produce in the garden, all the chores of the country life she cherishes, and which she contrives to have out of the way before any guest appears.

I turned my attention to the three books on the bedside table (an unmistakable touch), carefully selected and inviting, they spoke for him: 'I thought you might like these!' Indeed, the only problem was which to tackle first. Alec reads a great deal and his choices, while off-beat and unusual, always have been right and have never failed to divert me. It would be heaven to have him always – not only this day – as my own, special librarian, infallible and challenging.

Alec truly defines hospitality, and his warmth extends far beyond. I know he has been the first to help when fellow actors and friends have been down on their luck. He is distressed, sympathetic and encouraging when friends experience a failure of any kind. He is very enamoured of good acting, and of good actors when they are good.

His greatest gift to me on this occasion was the day itself. It was mine to do with as I pleased – no 'we have to go here, we have to go there.' He doesn't drive, nor does he beset one with places and people that have to be driven to.

It was one of those rare, halcyon English summer days that erase all the grey drizzle from the memory, and there were the immediate surroundings to enjoy. The entire house and its grounds bespeak everything about this generous, adorable and self-confessed odd couple. Built to their design at the start of their union of many years, it is an elegant delight.

Alec is an epicure. Great taste pervades both his work and life styles. He knows exactly what roles to select, has a canny perception for a good script, and is similarly astute as a connoisseur of art, literature, food and wine.

The idyllic garden, to which I made my way, owes much of its charm to the interests, rural hobbies and loving care of Merula. 'This England' in a nutshell!

I set about my selected reading. Books were considerably involving me, as my soul-mate (husband, actor Vincent Price) was detained by work in California. Happily, Vinnie shares my appreciation and love of Alec and Merula, and it is one of our delights on being in London to visit them. This time, Vinnie was not only missing, he was missing out.

Alec is well aware of the admiration and great affection I hold for Alan Bennett, the author of several of Alec's greatest theatrical moments. It is another of his sensitivities that he knows how to juxtapose his guests, and the only other visitor into that sun-dappled interlude was, by thoughtful design, our playwright friend.

With Alan arrived, made welcome and at his leisure, the two of us relaxed in the cool, afternoon shade. I asked Alan about his play, *The Old Country*, an outstanding success for Alec a few seasons before, concerning a defector to Soviet Russia. I had been inspired and enthralled by the performance, leaving the theatre with only one regret – the eternal one, still prevailing, that I have never had the joy and challenge of working with Alec.

Our host was at that moment off in the kitchen, cutting either his fingers or the bread as he contrived cucumber sandwiches, which certainly stretched his culinary prowess to the fullest.

I wanted to know if Alan had taken his spy characters from life. It was then that, after many years of promised silence, I first related my extraordinary encounter with Guy Burgess, an experience to which Alan was to apply his genius in realising it as *An Englishman Abroad*.

With Alec approaching our tree, the subject was dropped in favour of tea-time. However, the seed had been sown for a project that was to affect me so importantly, and, in looking back, it is rather appropriate that Alec was involved.

Here, he was the catalyst, but his counsel and guidance have proved life-saving therapies to me throughout our loving friendship. Most find their confidants by instinct, and my view of Alec as a wise shoulder to lean on proved a perceptive choice. We have the same religious belief (although I sense he is the more dedicated). The fact that he had been a convert to Catholicism like myself, and that this had had such a marked influence on his life, could explain why, for me, he is an ideal mentor.

I am not aware of any troubles that ruffle his serenity. However, I know his extraordinary letters – which provide my vital link with London, news of friends, little bits of gossip and theatre criticisms and occasional confidences – reveal a searching, emotional depth. Also, it is in this correspondence that his humour flourishes. Every one of his letters contains two or three laughs to provide me with pleasure on each reading.

However, I have never known him to laugh volubly, rather a silent amusement, his merriment contained to a mischievous smile. Nor have I seen him resort to mimicry – a favourite domain of most actors. His humour has the sharpness to devastate without that ploy.

He did recount to me recently a rare occasion when he employed that device.

Alec had just been cast for his latest screen assignment, an adaptation of *Little Dorrit*. He was waiting eagerly in the lobby of the Connaught for a re-union with a life-long friend. Seeing a familiar figure approach, he ducked behind a pillar, and, as the person drew level, he sprang out before him, and, in pixie abandon, proclaimed: 'Pst! Pst! It's Leetull Dawrit!' The tableau froze. Alec found himself confronted by a perfect stranger.

It was on such delicious anecdotes that we dined that evening, enjoyment enhanced by one of the very best martinis imaginable. The Guinness generosity, all dispensed with true affection, was not to end with our goodnights. On hand, was the local driver to accommodate a comfortable return to town.

Alec waved farewell to me and I looked back at him, framed in the doorway. His attire – cardigan and well-worn trousers – had been exactly right for this day in the country. But, I knew for sure that should our next encounter be anywhere in the city he would be head-to-toe immaculate. Mr Impeccable poses a constant problem for the likes of Jean Marsh,[1] Eileen Atkins and yours truly, when he invites us to lunch or dine, invoking: 'Oh, dear, what do

---

[1] Jean Marsh (b. 1938) actress; with Eileen Atkins devised the television series *Upstairs, Downstairs*.

we wear?' It is a true test of our respective savoir-faire, and I feel it is one we all relish.

All too swift to fly, that day in the country was complete, but by no means over. It is still with me, and richly cherished.

Even more importantly, Alec himself and all he means to me forever abides as an integral part of my life.

My husband has frequently said to me: 'When in doubt about almost anything, consult a dictionary.' I did just that in seeking to qualify the love Alec inspires in me. 'Love: an affection of the mind caused by that which delights; to feel affection for, delight in and admire.' Yes, that will do! That says it all!

MICHAEL
CODRON

Undoubtedly the leading West End impresario of the last thirty years. Born in 1930, he was educated at St Paul's and at Worcester College, Oxford. He has made a major contribution to the theatre by presenting in London the plays of Harold Pinter, Simon Gray, Tom Stoppard, Alan Ayckbourn, Alan Bennett, Michael Frayn – the list is long and impressive. His association with Alec Guinness goes back to *Wise Child* at Wyndham's Theatre in 1967.

HIS MOST ALEC
MICHAEL CODRON [1]

There are two or three stories I can tell about Alec Guinness which seem to me to illuminate both his personality and his talent. I am thinking particularly of *Habeas Corpus* by Alan Bennett, although it was not the first time I had presented Alec in the West End. He had appeared for me previously in *Wise Child* by Simon Gray, and *A Voyage Round My Father* by John Mortimer. In *Wise Child*, incidentally, I thought he showed terrific courage. He appeared for most of the play dressed as a woman, and at one performance, a man shouted out, 'Oh, Sir Alec, how could you!' Alec remained calm. But the happiest times we had together were when we did *Habeas Corpus* and that was because he was at his most Alec.

I had not presented a play of Alan Bennett's before, but due to some dispute with another management the play came to me – on John Mortimer's recommendation, I think – and I immediately decided to do it. Ronald Eyre[2] was to direct. The leading part was not yet cast and after various ideas were floated I suggested Alec. Alan and Ron reacted in the way almost everyone reacts when a big star is suggested: 'He won't do it, this is a company play, all the parts are equal, he's much too grand, he's very famous, we'll just be wasting time.' 'Let's try,' I said, 'there's no harm in trying.'

---

[1] In conversation with the editor.

[2] Director and writer. He has directed Guinness three times: in *Habeas Corpus*, *A Voyage Round My Father* and, most recently, *A Walk in the Woods*. He is also the writer and presenter of two TV series, *The Long Search* and *The Ages of Man*.

So we sent the play to Alec and he also immediately agreed to do it.

Almost from the very start – before rehearsals began – he was, well, at his most Alec. 'I don't think I am right for it,' he said. 'Why did you choose me? Why choose me? I can't do it, I'm not going to be good in it. And it isn't false modesty, it's the truth.' As a matter of fact, I don't think it ever is *false* modesty with Alec. The panic is genuine, arising, I suspect, out of deep and habitual insecurities. And it didn't stop there; it was virtually a continuous complaint, 'I can't do it, I'm not going to be any good, why did you choose me?' Then, there were his concerns about the title. 'We can't call it *Habeas Corpus*, nobody will understand it, and please let me out of it. I'm simply not going to be right for the part.'

By the time we started auditioning and interviewing other actors Ron, Alan and I believed that Alec was by then calmer and, apart from his concern about the Latin title, firmly committed to the enterprise. Even the fact that our first choice for the actress to play opposite him had turned the play down because she thought it was too rude did not seem to upset him unduly. But then one day, at an audition in the Lyric Theatre, Alec turned to us and said, 'Cold feet.' Alan was full of admiration. 'What a wonderful title. That's it. We'll call it *Cold Feet*. Thank you, Alec.' 'No, no, no,' Alec said. 'I've *got* cold feet.'

But, of course, he stayed with the play and rehearsals began. One evening, Alec, Ron, Alan and I dined together and during the course of the dinner Alec announced that he had decided not to end the play, as written, by just dying. Instead, he suggested, he would do a dance of death, a little dance of death. Alan was not pleased. 'That's not my play,' he said, 'I'd rather you didn't. I don't think it's in keeping.' To which Alec replied, 'I think it is in keeping and I beg you to let me try it.' Alan reluctantly agreed, but added, 'Well, all I can say is it won't be in the published version.' It was just one example of Alec's inspirational quality. His instinct for what will work and will not work is incredible. In this case he was proved triumphantly right. He has an unerring theatrical instinct. His dance of death was magical, haunting, just what was needed. And of course it is in the published text.

Habeas Corpus duly opened to wonderful reviews for the play, for Alec, for his little dance of death, for the director and the other members of the cast but then Alec seemed to be even more worried.

He thought everyone else was good in the play except him. Again, I don't think this was false modesty; it's just very Alec. He's genuinely reticent, yes, modest, and self-contained. And with the huge success of *Habeas Corpus* he gained in confidence. But, some time later, when I presented him in *A Family and a Fortune*,[1] he expressed doubts about bringing the piece into London. We did, of course, and had another success. His solicitousness to Margaret Leighton throughout the whole run was touching. He is a very endearing man.

One last thing, another insight into the way Alec works. *A Voyage Round My Father* by John Mortimer is, as the title suggests, autobiographical, centred on Mortimer's father who was a blind barrister. Alec agreed to play the part. During our first week at Brighton before we came to the Haymarket, Mortimer expressed a reservation about the way things were going. He thought Alec was too gentle at the beginning of the play. 'My father,' he said, 'was an angry man, consumed by inner anger at his blindness and I'm not getting any of that.' Alec was somewhat astonished. 'But surely,' he said, 'you can see the anger in the breakfast scene by the way I hit my egg.' Now, that's very Alec, to express a man's railing at the world by the way he taps his soft-boiled egg.

---

[1] By Julian Mitchell from the novel by Ivy Compton-Burnett.

PHOTOGRAPHS
BY
SNOWDON

1954

'I admire Sir Alec enormously both as an actor and as a human being, and have had the great pleasure of photographing him over the years.' In 1954 Alec Guinness sat for the first time for Tony Armstrong-Jones, as he then was (aged 24), in his studio in Pimlico.

1967. Alec Guinness as Mrs. Artminster in *Wise Child* by
Simon Gray.

1968

Macbeth at the Royal Court Theatre, 1966. Simone
Signoret played Lady Macbeth.

Hotel Paradiso by Feydeau, Winter Garden Theatre, London, 1956. ━━━━━━━━━━

Taken at a photo call on stage, published by the *Daily Express*

...in a rehearsal room, published by *Vogue*.

1985

MICHAEL NOAKES

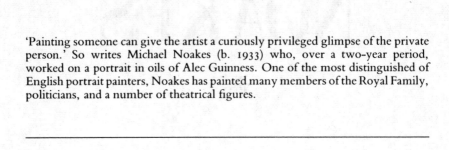

'Painting someone can give the artist a curiously privileged glimpse of the private person.' So writes Michael Noakes (b. 1933) who, over a two-year period, worked on a portrait in oils of Alec Guinness. One of the most distinguished of English portrait painters, Noakes has painted many members of the Royal Family, politicians, and a number of theatrical figures.

PORTRAIT
MICHAEL NOAKES

I worked on a portrait of Sir Alec during 1970 and 1971. It was an indication of his kindness that he really sat for my benefit, not for his own. It took quite a time because he was busy and sittings had to be spread out, and I did not make things easier by starting again several times. 'It's not surprising that you're taking so long,' people said at the time. 'This must be among your more difficult pictures. He's such a master of disguise. What do you think is the essential *him*?' An intriguing question. This book must provide a fascinating range of answers, for Guinness's character and personality are engagingly and delightfully complex.

To begin with, he has a marvellous ability to merge with the background when he wants to. He has developed his powers of observation to a very high level, and I imagine he finds more opportunity for adding to his visual storehouse if he avoids dominating a gathering. He could do so easily for, when he wishes to call on it, he has a powerful presence. He could make use of this and of the deference that people seem to accord naturally to the very famous, but he does not. He is among the least actorish of actors.

I think he has always regarded himself as a basic template on which he can extemporise – he enjoys playing around with hairpieces, for example, when on the stage or filming. People who know him only in performance probably never see the real Guinness, in the physical sense.

A portrait must aim to explore, of course, beyond this simple physical likeness, and painting someone can give the artist a curiously privileged glimpse of the private person. Guinness was prepared to talk to me about his early realisation that he was illegitimate and about his decision to become a Catholic, all now written about in his autobiography, *Blessings in Disguise*. I remember that I felt very complimented that he chose to tell me about these important factors in his life.

He has a strong visual sense, linked no doubt with those squirrelled-away observations he has gathered over the years. He worked very briefly in an advertising agency after he left school and, although it was as a copywriter, I think he had leanings towards painting and drawing even then. He makes delightful and rather Thurberesque caricatures, and I suspect that some of those anonymously-drafted Christmas cards that have arrived from the Guinness household over the years started life on his drawing board.

There was much talk about pictures. He had had a curious experience, which he later described in his autobiography as near-psychic, when he had one day felt threatened in some way by a Meninsky painting that he and his wife had in their bedroom. His mind filled with a verse from St Luke that seemed, ominously, to fit the scene: he observed tortured figures in the picture that he had not seen before. It obviously made him feel very uneasy, and he removed it from the wall. Later, they discovered that it was the anniversary of Meninsky's suicide. This, and his now well-known warning to James Dean that if the young man climbed into his brand-new car he would be found dead in it inside a week – a prophecy that was fulfilled – were powerful experiences for Guinness.

Less seriously, I recall him describing his sense of disquiet about a small landscape that he had bought. It puzzled him . . . something was wrong. What he perhaps feared was going to be another sinister experience turned out to have a prosaic explanation. Whoever had painted the picture had obviously lingered over it for too long on site without making adjustments for the changing light: the bushes in one corner had cast their shadows in one direction, the tree in the foreground was lit from the other side. The result had been strangely disturbing until he realised the reason. Then he was able to laugh at it.

In the portrait, wanting to give an indication of the busy interior life of Sir Alec, I painted him surrounded by more space than I would normally allow. It is dangerous for a painter to talk about his aims in a picture because the artist's ambitions for a work too easily exceed the ability to attain them, but my hope was that the lone figure would be read as shrewdly observing all that goes on around whilst knowing that it is all – the heights and the depths – the beating of a gnat's wing. Observing with humour, of course: but I think his humour is of that very high order, a cousin always of sadness, that is to do with a sense of proportion. That, after all, is one of the definitions of humour. It is closely linked to an appreciation of life's absurdities.

The most recent time I saw him was by chance. I was in my car, he was walking. It was summer, and he was wearing a large floppy hat and an overcoat. He carried a plastic bag in each hand, and was wandering up St James's Street looking as if he were searching for a taxi. I stopped my car and asked if I could give him a lift. So kind, no thank you, just looking for a particular turning-off. So kind. He must surely have taken pleasure from the knowledge that everyone who glanced at him without a thought would have been tickled pink to have known who he was, had he decided to be less anonymous.

Brooding on this, I realised that in a sense he must also have chosen to be eye-catching. There is a curious interplay of intentions here. In the introductory paragraphs to his autobiography he talks of an awareness of the pull between these two sides to his personality, for he claims there that he is equally attracted and repelled by the limelight: he chose to be an actor, with all the implications of that career, and yet he is one of the most modest of men.

I think this tension underlies all his best performances and gives them that unique quality that is special to him. Thank heavens for it.

GEORGE
LUCAS

George Lucas is the creator of the phenomenally successful *Star Wars* saga, the epic film adventures including *Star Wars*, *The Empire Strikes Back* and *Return of the Jedi*. Lucas is a graduate of the USC School of Cinema and Television, and his first film as director was *THX-1138* (1971). In 1973, he co-wrote and directed *American Graffiti*, and has since produced eleven films, including *Raiders of the Lost Ark* (1981), *Indiana Jones and the Temple of Doom* (1984), *Willow* (1988), and *Tucker, A Man and his Dream* (1988).

FRAME REVELATIONS

GEORGE LUCAS

I'm a screenwriter and a film director, not an anecdotalist, so my orientation is in images. When I think of the time spent working with Alec, I see him sitting in his chair on the set with an approachable, relaxed elegance. He always looked to me, sitting there, like he was on the deck of a ship on some exotic cruise floating down a celluloid river.

The biggest challenge I had in directing *Star Wars* was to make it believable; to make it absolutely credible and real for the two hours it would be projected in a dark room. In order to create this fabricated reality I needed actors who could take fantastic and impossible situations and infuse them with an almost documentary authenticity.

I needed Alec Guinness. I needed his talent, his professionalism, and his class. Alec brought a respectability to the project that inspired the cast, the crew, and the director.

It was an incredible blessing for me to have Alec play the master warrior Ben Kenobi. To have an actor of Alec Guinness's calibre meant a great deal in helping the other actors get into their roles. Their respect for his character was drawn from their respect for him in real life. He was an important influence on the set, particularly because I had a technical crew that wasn't completely understanding of the material. Not that Alec was able to make things any clearer, but his presence lent so much credibility that everyone finally believed that giant furry aliens and talking robots made perfect sense.

Having Alec treat the difficult task of making a special effects movie, where nothing is real and many of the characters were to be added later, with such serious effort and patience set a standard for everybody.

Exactly why Alec agreed to work in an off-the-wall space fantasy I'll never know. He said he didn't understand science fiction at all. But, in the end, he did understand his character perfectly and it was a tribute to his seemingly endless professionalism that he was able to throw himself into the film the way that he did. Most of the other actors in the film were relatively new and I think that they really benefited from the experience of working with him.

My scripts are not the most readable pieces of literature. They are visual blueprints designed to make a film, not sell a project. I was quite nervous when I submitted the project to Alec. And I was pleasantly surprised when he asked to meet me. He explained at lunch that he didn't really understand the script, and because I was so young and had only made two low-budget movies, he was not really familiar with my work. I was beginning to wonder why he had bothered to meet me, when he told me that he had asked the director he was currently working with about me, and fortunately, the director was a big fan of my films and gave me a high recommendation. Alec seems to put more faith in talent and people than he does in scripts. On this basis we hit it off very well and he subsequently agreed to do the film. I thought this was a bit of a miracle because I'm not much of a salesman. It may well have been Alec who said that I manage charm without inflection.

The biggest crisis between Alec and me occurred the week before shooting. I had been frantically rewriting the script during rehearsals. When I finished it, I took Alec to lunch in order to explain the new draft and some of the more pertinent changes I had made. Things seemed to go well as I explained how I had improved his character and dialogue. However, just as the main course arrived, I started to get into a small plot change, and I could tell by the look in his eyes this was going to be a meal that would be hard to digest. In the original screenplay, Ben Kenobi was introduced on page twenty and became the leader and tutor of a small band of rebels. He led them on a series of adventures that culminated in a giant space battle that destroyed the evil empire's principal weapon, the 'Death Star', and ended with Ben giving everyone medals. As I told Alec the important part of the plot change, I began to get a little nervous. 'Although Ben is the leader,' I explained, 'I think it might be better if he . . . oh, like kinda died halfway through the picture.' Well, Alec was understandably upset. People don't like dying, whether it be in life, in their dreams, or in a film; especially not halfway through the film, and particularly not over lunch.

After I had told him about his newly written premature demise, he was extremely civil towards me, but I could tell he was upset. Later, I received word from his agent that he no longer wanted to do the picture. I had a major anxiety attack and another long meeting with him. I went on and on about how important the change was in order to make the story work. And how important it was to have a powerful actor play Ben, especially now that he had so much less screen time. As a writer, he was easily convinced. As an actor it took a little more work, but eventually he came around and threw himself into the job as if there had never been a disagreement.

The most vivid image I have of Alec is a moment I caught on film by accident. We were filming a scene in the cockpit of Han Solo's spaceship. The area was cramped. Han was at the controls, the giant furry alien, Chewie, was sitting next to him in the co-pilot's chair, and Luke and Ben were standing, squeezed in right behind them.

It was a difficult scene and we had to film it over and over again. At one point during the scene, Chewie had to reach up and hit a switch above Alec's head. As sometimes happens in these situations, in one of the takes Chewie reached up to flip the switch for the umpteenth time and accidentally hit Alec right square in the face. Alec was unhurt but had been taken quite by surprise, and fell out of character. When I looked at the film the next day on the editing machine I noticed something interesting. When I took the film from the moment Alec was hit and studied it one image at a time, I saw Alec's face go through a series of different characters, all in a split second, starting with Ben and ending with Alec, with about a half dozen completely different characters in between.

Watching that moment, I came to understand more clearly the incredible physical nature of creating a character; how a truly gifted actor is so concentrated, so thorough that even their facial muscles are transformed. Like a chameleon, Alec has a lot of different shades, different colours and different characters. Every frame of film from the moment he was hit was a different character . . . bump, bump, bump, until he finally arrived where he originated . . . at a wonderfully talented actor named Alec Guinness.

EPILOGUE

EPILOGUE

Extract from a postcard to the editor: 6. V. 88

Dear Ron,

. . . wouldn't it be good to call the whole thing off? I must say I'd breathe more easily. I think one's friends find it embarrassing and others just a chore . . . I'd hate anyone to be pressurised. Why not wait until my (unlikely) 80th? I would be gaga by then and not notice and no one who knew me in my twenties likely to be alive. So there you needn't do it at all.

Affectionately,
Alec

The Prisoner, Globe Theatre, 1954. As the Cardinal with
Noel Willman as the Interrogator.

Hamlet, Old Vic, at the New Theatre, 1951.

As Jock Sinclair in *Tunes of Glory,* with John Fraser, 1960.

Ross, 1960. As Rattigan's Lawrence of Arabia.

Ben Kenobi in *Star Wars*, 1977

From the portrait in oils by Michael Noakes, completed in 1971. (See also back flap of jacket.)

William Dorrit in *Little Dorrit,* 1986

The Pope in *Brother Sun, Sister Moon*, 1973.

16A John le Carré's George Smiley, 1979 and 1981.

16B *A Walk in the Woods,* Comedy Theatre, 1988. As Andrey Brotvinnik, with Edward Hermann.

KEY TO THE FRONTISPIECE

by Clive Francis

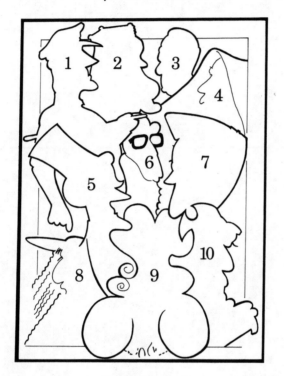

1–Colonel Nicholson, *The Bridge on the River Kwai*, 1957.
2–Prince Feisal, *Lawrence of Arabia*, 1962. 3–Adolf Hitler,
Hitler: The Last Ten Days, 1973. 4–Ben Kenobi, *Star Wars*, 1977.
5–Herbert Pocket, *Great Expectations*, 1946. 6–George Smiley,
Tinker, Tailor, Soldier, Spy, 1979. 7–Lady Agatha d'Ascoyne,
Kind Hearts and Coronets, 1949. 8–Fagin, *Oliver Twist*, 1948.
9–Charles I, *Cromwell*, 1970. 10–Professor Marcus, *The
Ladykillers*, 1955.

CHRONOLOGY

ALEC GUINNESS

Chronological table of parts and productions

1933

	Film	*Evensong*	Extra

1934

	Playhouse	*Libel!*	Junior Counsel
	Piccadilly	*Queer Cargo*	Chinese coolie, French pirate, English sailor
	New	*Hamlet*	Osric, Third Player

1935

	New	*Noah*	Wolf
	New	*Romeo and Juliet*	Sampson, Apothecary

1936

	New	*The Seagull*	Workman, then Yakov

1936–37

	Old Vic	*Love's Labour's Lost*	Boyet
	Old Vic	*As You Like It*	Le Beau, William
	Old Vic	*The Witch of Edmonton*	Old Thorney
	Old Vic	*Hamlet*	Osric, Reynaldo
	Old Vic	*Twelfth Night*	Sir Andrew Aguecheek

	Old Vic	*Henry V*	Exeter
	Elsinore	*Hamlet*	Osric, Player Queen, Reynaldo
1937–38			
	Queen's	*Richard II*	Aumerle, Groom
	Queen's	*The School for Scandal*	Snake
	Queen's	*The Three Sisters*	Fedotik
	Queen's	*The Merchant of Venice*	Lorenzo
	Richmond	*The Doctor's Dilemma*	Louis Dubedat
	Old Vic	*Trelawny of the 'Wells'*	Arthur Gower
	Old Vic	*Hamlet*	Hamlet
	Old Vic	*The Rivals*	Bob Acres
1939			
	Tour Europe and Egypt	*Hamlet*	Hamlet
	Tour	*Henry V*	Chorus
	Tour	*The Rivals*	Bob Acres
	Tour	*Libel!*	Emile Flordon
	Old Vic	*The Ascent of F.6*	Michael Ransom
	Perth	*Romeo and Juliet*	Romeo
	Rudolf Steiner Hall	*Great Expectations*	Herbert Pocket (and adaptor)
1940			
	Globe	*Cousin Muriel*	Richard Meilhac
	Old Vic	*The Tempest*	Ferdinand
	English tour	*Thunder Rock*	Charleston
1942			
	Henry Miller, New York	*Flare Path*	Fl. Lt. Graham
1945			
	Albert Hall	*Heart of Oak (pageant)*	Nelson
1946			
	Lyric	*The Brothers Karamazov*	Mitya (and adaptor)
	Arts	*Vicious Circle (Huis Clos)*	Garcin
	Film	*Great Expectations*	Herbert Pocket
1946–47			
	New	*King Lear*	Fool

	New	*An Inspector Calls*	Eric Birling
	New	*Cyrano de Bergerac*	De Guiche
	New	*The Alchemist*	Abel Drugger
1947–48			
	New	*Richard II*	Richard II
	New	*Saint Joan*	The Dauphin
	New	*The Government Inspector*	Hlestakov
	New	*Coriolanus*	Menenius Agrippa
	New	*Twelfth Night*	Director
	Film	*Oliver Twist*	Fagin
1949			
	Savoy	*The Human Touch*	Dr James Simpson
	Lyceum, Edinburgh	*The Cocktail Party*	Sir Henry Harcourt-Reilly
	Film	*Kind Hearts and Coronets*	The d'Ascoyne family
	Film	*A Run for Your Money*	Whimple
1950			
	Henry Miller, New York	*The Cocktail Party*	Sir Henry Harcourt-Reilly
	Film	*Last Holiday*	George Bird
	Film	*The Mudlark*	Disraeli
1951			
	New	*Hamlet*	Hamlet (and co-directed)
	Film	*The Lavender Hill Mob*	Henry Holland
	Film	*The Man in the White Suit*	Sidney Stratton
1952			
	Aldwych	*Under the Sycamore Tree*	The Ant Scientist
	Film	*The Card*	Denry Machin
1953			
	Shakespeare Playhouse, Stratford, Ontario	*All's Well That Ends Well*	King of France
	Shakespeare Playhouse, Stratford, Ontario	*Richard III*	Richard III

Film	*Malta Story*	Flight Lieutenant Peter Ross
Film	*The Captain's Paradise*	Henry St James
Film	*Father Brown*	Father Brown

1954

Globe	*The Prisoner*	The Cardinal
Documentary	*The Stratford Adventure*	Himself

1955

Film	*To Paris with Love*	Col. Sir Edgar Fraser
Film	*The Prisoner*	The Cardinal
Film	*The Ladykillers*	Professor Marcus
Documentary	*Rowlandson's England*	Narrator

1956

Winter Garden	*Hotel Paradiso*	Boniface
Film	*The Swan*	Prince Albert

1957

Film	*The Bridge on the River Kwai*	Colonel Nicholson
Film	*Barnacle Bill*	William Horatio Ambrose

1958

Film	*The Horse's Mouth*	Gulley Jimson (and wrote)

1959

Film	*The Scapegoat*	John Barrett, Jacques de Gue
TV	*The Wicked Scheme of Jebal Deeks*	Jebal Deeks

1960

Haymarket	*Ross*	T. E. Lawrence
Film	*Our Man in Havana*	Jim Wormold
Film	*Tunes of Glory*	Lieutenant-Colonel Jock Sinclair

1961

Film	*Majority of One*	Koichi Asano

1962

Film	*H.M.S. Defiant*	Captain Crawford
Film	*Lawrence of Arabia*	Prince Feisal

1963			
	Lyceum, Edinburgh	*Exit the King*	Berenger
1964			
	Plymouth, New York	*Dylan*	Dylan Thomas
	Film	*The Fall of the Roman Empire*	Marcus Aurelius
1965			
	Film	*Situation Hopeless – But Not Serious*	Herr Frick
	Film	*Doctor Zhivago*	General Yegraf Zhivago
1966			
	Phoenix	*Incident at Vichy*	Von Berg
	Royal Court	*Macbeth*	Macbeth
	Film	*Hotel Paradiso*	Boniface
	Film	*The Quiller Memorandum*	Pol
1967			
	Wyndham's	*Wise Child*	Mrs Artminster
	Film	*The Comedians*	Major Jones
1968			
	Chichester Festival Theatre, Wyndham's, Haymarket	*The Cocktail Party*	Sir Henry Harcourt-Reilly (and directed)
1969			
	TV	*Conversation at Night*	Executioner
1970			
	Yvonne Arnaud, Guildford	*Time Out of Mind*	John
	Film	*Cromwell*	Charles I
	Film	*Scrooge*	Marley's Ghost
	TV	*Twelfth Night*	Sir Andrew Aguecheek
1971			
	Haymarket	*A Voyage Round My Father*	Father
1972			
	TV	*Solo*	

1973			
	Lyric	*Habeas Corpus*	Dr Wicksteed
	Film	*Brother Sun, Sister Moon*	The Pope
	Film	*Hitler – The Last Ten Days*	Adolf Hitler
1974			
	TV	*The Gift of Friendship*	Jocelyn Broome
	TV	*Caesar and Cleopatra*	Julius Caesar
1975			
	Apollo	*A Family and a Fortune*	Dudley
1976			
	Queen's	*Yahoo*	Dean Swift (and co-author)
	Film	*Murder by Death*	Bensonmum
1977			
	Queen's	*The Old Country*	Hilary
	Film	*Star Wars*	Obi-Ben Kenobi
1979			
	TV	*Tinker, Tailor, Soldier, Spy*	George Smiley
1980			
	Film	*The Empire Strikes Back*	Obi-Ben Kenobi
	Film	*Raise the Titanic*	Bigalow
	Film	*Little Lord Fauntleroy*	Earl of Dorincourt
1981			
	TV	*Smiley's People*	George Smiley
1982			
	Film	*Lovesick*	Sigmund Freud
1983			
	Film	*Return of the Jedi*	Obi-Ben Kenobi
1984			
	Film	*A Passage to India*	Professor Godbole
	Chichester	*The Merchant of Venice*	Shylock
1985			
	Film	*Monsieur Quixote*	Monsieur Quixote
1986			
	Film	*Little Dorrit*	William Dorrit

1987

Film	*A Handful of Dust*	Mr Todd

1988

Comedy	*A Walk in the Woods*	Andrey Botvinnik

INDEX

INDEX